SALT OF A SAILOR

ANNIE DIKE

Salt of a Sailor

Table of Contents

Prologue...5

One About Your Boat 9

Two Roughing It..15

Three There Goes the ColorStay.......................29

Four 93.46 Perfect...51

Five Survey(or) Says ... .69

Six You Mean, You and I, We?.........................83

Seven By the Moon 101

Eight By the Stars 117

Nine Surely Loctite Can Fix This 129

Ten Mattresses and Parachutes? That's Crazy Talk 151

Eleven Who Has the Gorton Pants? 163

Twelve Non-Drowsy My Ass 185

Thirteen I'm Getting Sparks 201

Fourteen Right of the River.............................. 209

Fifteen Did He Say Curly Fries?....................... 225

Sixteen A Dasani Bottle and Some Duct Tape.............. 241

Seventeen Team Docking 259

Eighteen Best Sail of Our Lives........................ 269

Nineteen The Joys of Boat Ownership 279

Twenty The REAL Joys of Boat Ownership...................... 307

Twenty-One About Your Boat 319

About the Author 323

Prologue

I don't care if I've heard it a hundred times, twice last week and once yesterday, every time he starts, I can't help it. I can't hide it, and I can't stop it. I smile. He often tells it as he's shoving a thick, furry wad of black tobacco under his lower lip, and I smile as he does. I smile because I know where I'm going. I've been there, plenty of times, but I don't care. I know what I'm going to see along the way, what I will smell, taste and feel. I know I will hang on every word and feel that same hot pulse of excitement I always do when he looks to me occasionally to see if I know what's coming. I do, but I never let on. I just follow him. My dad is taking me. So I go.

Dirt cakes in the deep crevices of his neck. A fat drop of sweat rolls out from his frayed gray hair, navigates its way over each skin crevice and soaks into the stained collar of his ragged yellow shirt. My dirty thighs stick out of cut-off jeans and sweat on the rough, dry upholstery of the bench seat. Huge chunks are torn out in places exposing the weird yellow foam that I just can't help but pick at. If Grandaddy asks I'll deny I did it, but my pockets are full of little pieces of yellow fluff. I can taste the dust from the country road. I squint into the sun, look at the rumpled papers stuck under the visor, watch the leather keychain that hangs and swings on the shifter arm. I am there. Sitting in the dusty cab of Granddaddy's rusted-out blue 1942 Ford pick-up. I'm somewhere around the age of eight and I'm bumping along the rutted country road with my Granddaddy to Willingham's feed store to pick up a sack of feed.

I'm there because my dad has put me there. He has constructed this dusty, scratchy scene around me so that I can't see anything else. I have become him. I am in that truck, looking at his Grandaddy's neck, picking a wad of seat foam behind my back. I often unconsciously pick at the couch or whatever cushion I'm sitting on out of instinct when dad talks about the weird yellow foam because it's such a great detail. I'm picking and riding and choking on the country dust. I know I'm going to get a penny candy at the store and that Granddaddy's going to get a can of snuff. He pinches off a wad and packs it in his gums before he even makes his way to the counter to sign the store credit slip for Hattie Willingham, "Miss Hattie" to the regulars. He mulls the thick wad around in his mouth as he opens the rickety door to the truck, groans his way back into the pick-up seat, and then launches a thick stream of black juice out the window by the fuel pump before leaving.

"But, one time, *this time!*" my dad says. His grandfather got in the truck, slammed the metal door, slowly rolled the window up, and spat a huge tobacco burst onto it. My dad will tell you it splat loudly on the glass and dripped down like coffee in cane syrup and that his grandfather said and did nothing. He didn't even flinch from the back-splash. "Grandaddy just rolled the window back down," my dad's arm slowly cranking down an imaginary window. Slowly. "Spat and all," still

rolling. "Like it never even happened." *See?* That's the good part, the reason I smile, the reason I never let on I know what's coming and the reason I never get tired of that one. It's a great story because it's a small event–a seemingly tiny, miniscule happening–that my dad crafted into a big story, pregnant with imagery, detail and–my favorite–humor. And, because it's told by a great story-teller: "Tricky Dickey" himself, my Old Man.

When the Captain and I set off on this quest, I knew each day and each adventure we endured, both on and off the boat, would have all the makings of a great story if only it were to fall in the hands of a great story-teller. From the smallest, most miniscule of events–a tobacco splat on a window, if you will, to the epic, deadly tangles at sea—each experience would have the potential to capture and entertain. As long as I could expertly construct the scene, with sights, sounds and weird foam details, then you would see, smell and taste nothing else. You would be there with us on that salty, swaying boat, experiencing each of our glorious undertakings and our likely more plentiful mistakes. From finding our boat to making the initial harrowing trek across the Gulf of Mexico in it, we certainly gathered many stories worth telling, some truths too. These are just a few.

ONE

About Your Boat

"The police?" Phillip asked, his face a mix of worry and amusement. I mouthed the word at him but he shrugged it off. Surely he was just jacking me around. *The police?* I wasn't buying it.

"Well, you didn't tell them where I was, did you?" he said with a nervous laugh. His laugh caught me. Stopped me. This wasn't a show for my benefit. Whoever he was talking to was *really* talking about the police. They were *really* after him. I now watched Phillip closely as he asked a few more questions, paced around in a tight circle and gave me a heck-if-I-know look. Surely someone was jacking *him* around, though. *Seriously? The police?*

We were in New York City at the time. In all of my thirty years, I had never been and, much to Phillip's delight, I imitated the Pace Picante commercial repeatedly in the weeks before the trip. Anytime anyone asked, "Where you going, Annie?" I would reply, "New York Ci-teee!" with an exaggerated country drawl and bug eyes. I said I was thirty. I didn't say I was mature. Besides, it was the first time I could use that played-out commercial tagline meaningfully. Who wouldn't? We had been planning the trip for months, plotting our attack on the

9

city, reading dozens of travel guides and books, making reservations, then canceling those and making better ones! We were really excited about the ci-teee. And, wouldn't you know it—of course—Mother effin Nature decided to drop Tropical Storm Karen on us the *very* weekend we were set to leave. Perhaps she'd been planning her trip for months too. Making reservations at the marinas down in Miami, or perhaps Corpus Christi, then canceling those and deciding to drop right in on freaking Pensacola. It looked like she had her sights set right on our boat. *That bitch!*

Karen was a real pre-trip buzz-kill. The night before we left for NYC, we spent the entire evening tying and re-routing extra dock lines to keep the boat secure. We even lashed her to city property! We wrapped extra towels and padding around the places where we thought the lines might rub (chafe guards they call them), bungeed and strapped down any material or canvas we thought might go to flapping, which meant blowing right off. We got her as secure as we could get her, lined up some buddies to check on her in our absence and left. Karen was way out in the Atlantic at the time, and we had reservations!

And, here we were by the Flatiron Building, walking off two Shake Shack burgers and three glasses of wine. One for Phillip. Two for me. They serve an exceptional red at the Shack. Goes great with the burgers. I had that half-tipsy feeling that makes you crinkle your nose up a little just to check the numbness of it and then smile to yourself because you're the only one who knows what you're doing and why. Or, so you think. But, secretly, the thought of getting called out for nose-crinkling makes you smile too. Needless to say, I wasn't mentally prepared for this latest turn of events. *The police? For real?*

"The police," Phillip said to me, as if he'd heard my litany of thought-questions and was answering them aloud, but his statement was still more of a question than an answer. "I have no freaking clue."

He shook his head. "I," he started then stopped, huffed half-annoyed and started again. "I … I don't know. I can't even imagine …" Phillip trailed off, staring at his phone in disbelief. "I'll have to make some more calls. That was Linda at the office. She called me right after they left. They said they'd been to my house too. This guy," he said with disdain. "Some lieutenant and his beefed-up sidekick just showed up asking for me. He didn't say why." Phillip threw his hands up in frustration. "He just left a card. Said he couldn't … *disclose.*" Phillip was shaking his head now, punching in more numbers.

I flicked my nose back to feeling and sobered up three notches. *Holy shit. He was serious. The police!* It seemed it was a good thing we were in New York City, a far cry from home, because the heat was hot back in Pensacola. Soon, a scratchy voice came through the phone. Phillip was talking to some raspy, chain-smoking bloke, Sergeant So-and-So. The sidekick. Apparently he and the lieutenant had gone out to Phillip's house that morning and then to his office, trying to find him. Phillip tightened his jaw and avoided my stare. I wondered if he wasn't thinking about hanging up right then and there and making plans to stay in NYC for good. For whatever reason, the police were hot on his trail back home. The sidekick told us Lieutenant Whoever was out of the office at the moment but that he would have him call Phillip as soon as he got back.

We couldn't wait that long.

"Sergeant," Phillip waded in, "can I ask what all of this is about?" We waited through a silence while the sarge did something, probably swallowing the last bite of a greasy McSomething and wiping his mouth. Finally, a shuffle and rattle, and he responded.

"It's about your boat."

Your boat. Our comprehension came slowly, clumsily. *His boat? Wait. Did he mean our boat? The sailboat? Our boat!?*

Sickening thoughts started running through my mind. I imagined the boat had come untied in the storm winds, knocked out half the docks in the marina and ended up speared through the hull of the million-dollar catamaran in the last slip. Phillip cupped his hand over the phone, pushed it away from his face briefly and whispered, "The rails?" shrugging his shoulders at me. *The rails.* In an effort to secure her as best we could before leaving, we *had* tied the boat to the rails along the public seawall next to our dock. Perhaps the city was going to have to untie them with the coming storm? Or worse, perhaps they already *had* untied her, and they were calling to let us know that when they did, she rocked and swayed and came crashing into the city seawall. *Those bastards!*

"My, my ... boat?" Phillip finally stammered, jolting me back to reality, back to New York, back to the phone and Sergeant So-and-So's voice on the other end of the line. "What do you mean, my boat?"

"I'm sorry, mister, that's all I can disclose right now. You'll need to speak to the lieutenant when he gets back."

All he could disclose. *Disclose?* Like it was some big matter of national security or something? What the hell had our boat run into? A top-secret nuclear missile silo? Disclose. That word really pissed us off. As if when a cop has something to say, it no longer becomes "tell" it magically transforms into the utterly important "disclose."

Phillip and I wandered aimlessly around the park by the Flatiron, staring at his phone, willing it to ring while we waited for Lieutenant Whazzisname to call us back. We offered each other possible not-so-bad scenarios, but we both suspected the worst—the crashed, cracked versions. We kept turning his words over and over in our minds: "It's about your boat." How worried we were, I simply cannot *disclose.*

But, forgive me. I've gotten way ahead of myself. This was New York in October. In order to get a call "about our boat," we had to first *have* a boat, which required we find her, buy her and sail her home across the Gulf of Mexico. That was months earlier. We'll get there, don't worry.

Where did all of that mess begin? Where most promising messes do: late one night at a bar.

TWO

Roughing It

"The Grenadines," Phillip said. Casually, as if it was like going to the movies or out for a bagel. The way he said it made them sound closer. He made all things faraway sound closer.

"For how long?" I asked, kicking myself immediately right after I did. Like I was some lovesick school girl. *Summer camp? How long will you be gone Billy? Will you write?*

"Ten days," he replied. *Ten days*, I thought. And, just like some lovesick schoolgirl, the thought made me want to pout. I had only just met this man and I could already tell that ten whole days without him might feel like a small form of torture.

"Ten days," I repeated, not knowing what else to say. I had never met a man who had been to the Grenadines. I had never met a man who traveled at all, really (other than up to the hunting camp), much less a man who did it consistently and to such far-flung places. I had never met a man quite like him and, trust me, in the reckless months that led up to him, I had met plenty. Phillip was curious, but a bit dismissive, of me. Me, the leggy blonde who usually lorded over the fraternity brothers and navy boys at the bar with ease. A friend who knew I had wasted far too much time already with those types encouraged me to upgrade from "the toddlers" to a man like Phillip. Like me Phillip was newly single, but where I was running around like those kids in the Willy Wonka factory–snatching, tasting, and trying everything–he was sort of cooly sashaying about. Like a cat, his indifference made me crave his attention even more. Among the dopey, bounding dogs who often circled me, he stood out. Phillip was educated, put-together, capable of conversing about things other than the Alabama game. The man exuded so much confidence it rubbed off on you. He was also a lawyer, like me, but not the overly-cocky kind I was used to. He was assured but in no way judgmental. You got the sense that every man or woman who walked up to him–slick pin-striped corporate type to a dirty homeless beggar–would get the same handshake.

When he first walked up to me, the phrase, "I'll have what he's having," came to mind. After just a few minutes of focused conversation I was enthralled by him. Phillip was direct, almost to the point of being off-putting. If he had something to say, he would say it. If he didn't, he would say nothing. I struggled with it at first–unsure whether I should interpret his frequent silence as disinterest–but I soon recognized it merely as a strong sense of self. Words were not wasted between us. It was unnerving, almost, how quickly we fell into an ease of honesty and companionship. "What he's having" soon evolved into "Where he's going." The man was so traveled. Phillip had been to Kuwait, Somalia, Singapore, and now the Grenadines? I couldn't point these places out on a map, but I certainly didn't want him to know that. I didn't want to risk asking a question that would reveal my lack of knowledge about in which hemisphere, or even what ocean, the Grenadines lie—assuming it was an ocean, not a sea or a gulf or whatever the correct term for those rare bodies of water that exist out there in the great beyond. The Grenadines. For some reason, an image of Desert Storm came to mind—dust, tents in the desert, chickens clucking around—and I knew instantly it had to be wrong. So very wrong.

"Well, probably seven days on the boat. Ten days total for the whole trip." Thankfully, he had brushed the desert dust away and brought me back to the bar. I was hoping the more he spoke, the more I would become enlightened, but now I was only further confused, intrigued, enraptured. *On the boat? What boat? Whose boat? What kind of boat?* Desert Storm flashed again, and I stabbed in the dark, hoping out of the thick froth of my confusion would emerge an intelligent question.

"Your boat?"

"No, a friend's. I'm going to stay with them on their boat for about a week in the Grenadines." *Whew, a relevant inquiry. Don't blow it , Annie.* But, as hard as I was trying to focus on our exchange, to say the right things, ask the right questions, I was swept away again by the words that tumbled off his lips. The Grenadines … they sounded so exotic. How could I carry on a conversation with this man? I was a lawyer, sure. I had a degree and whatnot, and had clawed my way up from dirt-poor beginnings, but I still had the dirt under my fingernails to prove it. Among my hoity-toity peers I often felt that I knew only just enough to pretend to know a lot. A quick wit and disarming personality can be just that—disarming. *As they scramble to get their armor back together, they'll forget to peek under mine.* When it came to dirty, rugged life experiences, I was rich, but as for world travel— real out-there, beyond-the-great-beyond travel—I was still dirt-poor. I knew nothing of these foreign places, these remote adventures, these …

"Another martini?" Thankfully, I was rescued again. This time it was the bartender.

"Yes, please, and a cosmo as well, extra lime." The words came out before I even had time to think about it.

Phillip eyed me curiously. Watching me as I knocked the last splash of my first martini back and met his gaze. My eyes squinting ever so slightly. *What?* they said.

"A cosmo *and* a martini?" he asked, now seemingly intrigued by me. Me? The one imagining chickens pecking at dirt when he said the Grenadines. *Good,* I thought. Finally, back on familiar turf. Booze and sultry flirting from a pretty blonde at the bar. Since the divorce, I was the queen of that realm. I didn't know how to compete with the Grenadines, with ten days abroad, friends with sailboats, remote, exotic locations, anything of that kind. But, I did know I liked this man, and I now had his attention—in my arena, on my turf. Time to break out the catnip.

"Sure. Salty *and* sweet," I quipped. "I like everything," I added suggestively, a gleam dancing in my eyes. "You ever find yourself in need of a hot blonde number to start making these trips to the … *Grenadines* and whatnot with you, you know where to find her." I brushed my body against his, reaching for my fresh martini and licking a salty bead from the rim before taking my first sip.

I watched him watch me, thinking he wasn't sure exactly what to say. What the appropriate response would be. Or so I imagined what he was thinking. But, as the seconds passed, us eyeing each other easily, in comfortable silence, I could tell he wasn't worried at all about what was appropriate. He was simply enjoying the moment. Pondering me. He smiled—a genuine, sexy smile—raised his own glass of some dark liquor with a sliver of lemon, and tipped it at me with a regal nod of his head. *Touché.*

I kid you not—that was our first exchange. The night we met there was talk of a sailboat and the Grenadines. That evening, I was poised to set sail to southern climates and salty, sweet adventures before our relationship had even begun. I was twenty-nine, freshly divorced and running like a wild stallion when Phillip met me, jumping and bucking in the vast freedom I had recently found, unsure what to do with it all. Molding it into a boat and sailing it with him down to the Grenadines sounded like a great start. But I was the easy sell. Being a bit more cautious and still smarting from his own separation, it took Phillip some time to grow comfortable with the fact that he might find himself again spending every day with the same person or the more frightening thought–that he *wanted* to. But, once he wised to my awesomeness and realized I truly wanted no commitment, we started to get serious about it. And, I do mean *it,* not each other. I'm not sure, still, if what we have could or should be called serious, or called anything for that matter.

What we got serious about was this sailing stuff, which was simply the embodiment of our mutual desire to spend our youthful days together, doing the things most put off until retirement. For us, that was to travel and experience the world, to embrace the excitement of living a different day every day. We had both put in several hard years at the office and it was time to come up for air. The Grenadines only fueled a fire that was already smoldering in Phillip. He had wanted his own boat for years. Not just any boat—a sailboat—a comfortable, dependable blue water cruiser that would take him anywhere he wanted to go. He didn't want to wait until he got old and arthritic to get out there. We were somewhat established professionally, both with some money saved up and still with our health and thirst for adventure. The right time to go was now. We made the mutual decision to adjust our careers accordingly and start getting ruthless with how we spent our time and money. It all needed to be devoted to the higher goal. Money was traded in for more time and the spare time was spent readying ourselves for world travel. While I am confident Phillip would have bought and sailed a boat on his own at that point in his life, cue Annie or not, the fact that a vivacious little budding world traveler crashed into his life around the same time was an undeniable impetus. Having a comfortable, dependable mate to accompany him would naturally make the journey more enjoyable. Wouldn't hurt if she was pretty to boot, but that wasn't a requirement.

Now, what did I want? Everything, in a sense, but not the usual one. I had just clawed my way out of a consuming marriage and I wanted to be free, free to go, write, and travel. I wanted to see the world, and have a kickass time doing it. I wanted to ski, climb, kiteboard, scuba dive.

And, sail? Sure sail! That too. Anything too. I wanted to do it all—to immerse myself everyday in the new, the now, and the never-before seen. And, Phillip, with his equally insatiable thirst for adventure (and, okay, his devilishly good looks), did not just "step into my life" at that time. He hit it, full on, with the force of a Mac truck, crashing into me at the perfect time and sending me skidding and careening onto a new road that was paved with adventure. I gripped the wheel, hugged the asphalt, shifted gears and took off. I was infected by Phillip the moment I met him. Where he was going, I wanted to go. And go we did. After a year or so of various escapades and non-sailing trips together, Phillip finally began to suspect what I had known that first night over cocktails and talk of the Grenadines. *She could be the one. Not* that *one—a way* better *one.* The "hot little blonde number" who would accompany him to "the Grenadines and whatnot." His travel mate! *Hadn't I told him that, on Night One? What more did he need?*

Proof, apparently. It seemed Phillip wanted some empirical evidence. He does like to test me, and for good reason. If you're going to travel the world with someone, you want to be sure they can hack it. Phillip wanted to be sure I packed light and traveled well, that I assimilated with ease into different environments, cultures and the occasional dirty, stuffy place. I had to be up for hiking, biking, backpacking and a variety of ethnic culinary experiences. Personally, I believe he was trying to make sure I wasn't a finicky, high-maintenance broad. Can't say that I blame him. There are plenty of them out there. After his own personalized series of "test trips," Phillip was finally starting to think I might fit the bill. I traveled with ease, ate happily of whatever was plated before me, and went with the flow. But this whole sailing business was new territory. There's just really no way to know what kind of sailor you'll turn out to be until you actually get out there and start doing it. I didn't even know how to sail. I'd never done it. What if I got violently seasick? I had been out a time or two on a deep-sea fishing trip and had had no problems, but that was it. But that was as a passenger on a motor yacht, not a deckhand on a swaying, to-and-fro sailboat—cruising was a whole 'nother matter, Phillip would tell me. Like camping, but on the water. Cruisers had to be ready to get their hands dirty, to endure some—or perhaps a lot—of discomfort. To "rough it" as some might say. It could be hard, painful and exhausting. You had to be resourceful, rough-and-tumble, decidedly not dainty—that was his gist. *I'm all of those things*, I told myself. *Hell, I'm the poster child for those things.* I had to smile when Phillip showed me pictures, had me read articles and tried to re-create sailing conditions or situations that he thought might help prepare me for this "tough" world of marine camping. They paled sadly in comparison to my past experiences—my tomboy resumé, if you will— my own "roughing it" days.

I really do think it is in my blood because it all started with my dad—a real-life, no-shit professional bull rider in his day, twelfth in the nation at one point, or so I was told—a true grit-and-gristle cowboy to the core. His daddy was a Church of Christ preacher and his momma, Big Mom, was the stubbornest, cattle-driving, child-rearing Southern stickler I've ever met. She was far tougher than dad, far tougher than any of us. As a child, I spent my summers in the Alabama

backwoods as dad's shadow, stumbling behind his spurs everywhere he went. Going everywhere my dad went often meant squeezing into hay trailers, climbing fences, holding onto the horn, holding on for dear life and, basically, just clawing the dirt to keep up. I did what he did, whatever that entailed. The rest of the year, my brother, John, and I spent in New Mexico with my mom, the stubbornest, bus-driving, child-rearing *non*-Southerner I've ever met, not quite as tough as Big Mom, but twice as mean when she needed to be.

With dad granted the fun summers-and-holidays role, my mom was left with the job of actually raising my brother and me, day in, day out, mostly alone and mostly broke. She was a hard-core disciplinarian, a great whipper and, despite the daily frustrations of raising two snot-nosed kids, a stern teacher and constant provider. Complaining was not tolerated in our little flat-top orange house in New Mexico. Gripe about mom not buying the sugary "Tiger" cereal you got at So-and-So's house and you spent your Saturday morning chained to the kitchen table, swallowing tasteless lumps of Malt-O-Meal, with absolutely no sugar or butter in it, until every last malt morsel was gone. "Some kids don't get breakfast at all," she would say. And, she was right. But, having little forced John and me to be creative, to construct our own worlds of entertainment, to build things we couldn't buy, to fix things others would throw away and to appreciate and save the seventy-five cents mom would give us for cleaning the bathroom (yes, *the* bathroom— growing up in our house, there was only one).

If I cursed her at the time—and believe me, thanks to my brother, I started cursing at a young age—it's only because I was ignorant. I was young, naive and stupid, and I didn't understand the valuable life lessons my mom was teaching us. Her tough love laid a thick salt base that enabled my brother and me to grip and grow in the face of adversity, poverty, and sometimes insurmountable odds. With this foundation, I was able to endure a young life full of experiences that humbled me, taught me, and made me this poster-child exemplar of toughness that I thought I was, this pre-seasoned storm trooper who could handle any nautical crisis. Now, had I ever sailed? No. Did I think that mattered? No. I had endured many painful, uncomfortable, arguably dire situations that I felt gave me whatever grit and guile the Captain thought I needed to handle this silly sailing stuff. The more Phillip kept trying to impress upon me how tough it was going to be, the more I kept reaching back to the rough-and-tumble memories of my youth, some of which Phillip knew about, most he did not.

But, they were mine. They were logged in and itemized, lined up on a mental shelf, standing ready for when I needed to pull one down, roll it around in my mind and embrace, once again, whatever valuable lesson I had learned in that moment. Big Mom, holding me down in a vat of hydrogen peroxide, my skin literally sizzling off, had taught me no matter how awful things may seem, if they're not going to kill you, they're not really that bad. "Awww hush," she'd say. "You're alive ain't ya?" My dad—pulling my head back with a wad of my hair in one hand and a pair of greasy pliers in the other to extract the wiggly, bloody tooth out of my mouth—had taught me, "It might hurt at the time, but sometimes you gotta cut things loose, if they're wanting to go." My brother, John—punching holes in canned biscuit dough and dropping them in the Fry Daddy to make our own homemade version of donuts—had taught me that if you really want something, particularly if folks say you can't have it, you find a way. In all, I felt I had already endured a lifetime's worth of "roughing it" experiences that made me far more durable than the average bloke. I had parachuted with a sheet, started my car with a screwdriver, swished with hydrogen peroxide. I rode horses, climbed rocks, leapt off cliffs. I fixed things with duct tape, staples and hot glue. I spent summers in the sleeper of a big rig. I ate Malt-O-Meal. Surely these were excellent traits for a sailor. Surely I was "salty" enough? I fancied I was. Phillip suspected I could be. Either way, we were going to find out. Travel was the goal. The time to go was now. All we needed was a boat.

THREE

There Goes the ColorStay

"Check it out. They're here," Phillip said, his face lit like a kid pressed to a toy store window display. It was books, a whole stack of them, wrapped in brown butcher paper, some in yellow bubble envelopes, others in boxes. There were at least six of them piled up by the door. Phillip hoisted them inside and started tearing into them. They were sailing books—books on sail trim, storm tactics, knot tying, diesel engine mechanics, voyagers' handbooks, travel guides, galley cookbooks—Nigel Calder, Beth Leonard, the Pardeys, you name it. Phillip had ordered a pile of them. While Phillip had sailed and crewed on many boats—he knew how to sail—he had never owned a boat of his own. This was going to be the first time the entire boat, the sails, the engine, the tanks, the electronics, every system on that boat, was going to be *his*, his job to monitor and maintain, his responsibility to ensure they all remained in working order. He craved knowledge.

"No matter how much you know about sailing, there is always more to learn, and every boat's different," Phillip explained to me. He had been researching boat designs, boat layouts, performance, quality, the pros and cons, and started scouring boat listings on the internet. Boats, like everything else in the world you might want, can be found on the worldwide web. They are listed pretty much like cars—on dealers' websites, brokers' websites, even craigslist. But, a boat is not like an L.L. Bean sweater or a coffee pot. It's soon to be your mistress. I would recommend you approach it like online dating: make sure you have all the compatibility points, but don't trust that profile pic.

While Phillip was tasked with the job of searching for our boat, I was tasked with the job of learning—learning how to sail a boat, how to steer a boat, how the boat functioned, learning boat layout, boat operation, boat performance, boat this, boat that. I knew nothing! I had a ton of crap to learn, and I was a bit overwhelmed. *Tanks, an engine, electronics? You mean, it's not just sticks and canvas?* The way Phillip described it, the boat was like an RV that floated. I began imagining a septic tank on the boat. *Where the hell did that go?* There were also water tanks, a sink, an oven, and fans. There were outlets and things that turned on and off with switches. There was a whole panel of things to turn on and off. *How in the world?* I was intrigued by this little, habitable home on the water. But I had yet to set foot on a single sailboat. While Phillip was learning too, he at least had context, some experience with all of these things. He knew, basically, where the systems were located and what they did. For me, it was all strictly theory—drawings and diagrams in textbooks. Phillip tried to explain things in different ways, use household items to demonstrate certain systems or point them out when we would walk through marinas. After a long day of briefs, oral arguments, phone calls and emails, we would swap our professional garb for shorts and boat shoes, walk the docks and chatter all evening about boat this and boat that. I remember how abruptly Phillip stopped walking one night when I asked him why people didn't raise their sails *before* they motored out of the slip. "You know, so it would already be done," I said. I don't think he even tried to hide his mortification. Phillip was as patient as he could be, and I was trying my darndest to soak it all during the evenings, then set it aside every day back at the office. Soon, though, the excitement and newness of the sailing stuff started to take precedence. I wanted to learn, and it irritated me that it was taking me so long and I was asking so many dumb questions along the way. *Raise their sails before they got out ...* I was trying, I swear. Everything was just so foreign to me.

Phillip and I sat many evenings while dinner was cooking, propped up side by side on the couch, reading countless textbooks, manuals, and handbooks on sailing, but he proved to be a far better student than I. While I am disciplined and do like to learn new things, it just doesn't really soak in unless I've got my hands and eyes on it and can see for myself how it works. A book can talk about the swing radius of a vessel on anchor and how to calculate it, but the words on the page don't really capture or convey the importance of it. Once I finally got out on the boat and anchored, I realized the swing radius is actually the distance your boat can go before it smacks into another boat, punctures its hull and sinks, or before it hits the bottom, tips over and sinks. *Ahhh ... now I get it.* Reading the books, I simply had no context for all of those diagrams and arrows. Plus, most of those books were so boring. I'm sorry, they just were. Their swing radius diagrams were just lines and arrows. They should have included little stickman sailors on the boat, their little stick arms flailing about and fret marks above their heads, right before their stick boat smashed into something. *Then* I might have gotten it. The best way I found to absorb some of these things was to mentally draw them, make up a little ditty or rhyme to remember or, if I could, match them to some experience in my past that made sense of them in my churning, country brain.

"That's the inner forestay." Phillip was pointing to a picture in a sailing book. "Some boats have an inner forestay permanently mounted and they run a smaller, staysail on it that they sail with most of the time. That's called a cutter rig. Other boats don't have the inner forestay set up permanently. They just rig it up when they think they might need to run a smaller sail, like for a storm or something. That's called a sloop." *A cutter rig, an inner forestay, a staysail, a sloop,* I repeated in my mind, trying to memorize all of this crap and figure out why it was important that I learn it. Not to mention why Phillip insisted on teaching me in the language I wasn't yet versed in. Why couldn't he call the mast the big pole that sticks up out of the boat—just until I got it? It was like trying to teach someone Spanish while only speaking Spanish. Thankfully, though, I had read and memorized enough to at least know what the "stays" were—wires that hold the mast up. When you draw a little stick diagram of a sailboat (and yes, I drew many a mental stick diagram in the beginning), you usually put a little half-moon boat shape on the bottom, then the mast sticking up from the center with a triangle sail on it. The forestay is a wire that runs forward—the direction known as "fore" on a boat, from the top of the

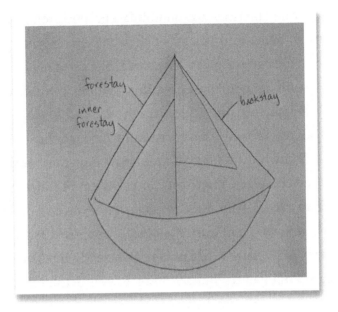

mast down to the foremost tip of your half-moon, the bow—and pulls the mast forward. The backstay counterbalances that, running from the top of the mast backward, known as "aft" on a boat, back to the end tip of your half-moon, known as the stern. So, an inner forestay wasn't so hard for me to process. It was a smaller line running, just like the forestay, from the mast down to the deck but just inside of the forestay, hence the name—inner forestay. *You see? This silly sailing stuff. Not so hard.*

But, I wasn't sure why I needed to know that the difference between a cutter and a sloop rig is that the inner forestay on the cutter is permanent and on the sloop it is not. *So what?* I imagined the primary reason you learn the names of different rigs was to enable you, when you walked around marinas, to congratulate properly other yachtsmen on the quality, build, and beauty of their vessels. "My my, Captain. That sure is a fine cutter rig you have there. She certainly looks yar."

"The reason it's good to know this," Phillip continued—*Thank goodness*, I thought, because other than the yar yachting commentary, I had no freaking clue why we were running through this—"is because you need to know the systems. If you know how they work and the purposes they can serve, then you can use them in different ways to serve different needs." *Wait, hold the phone. Now you lost me*, I thought. *You mean you want me to learn how they're* supposed *to be used, so I can use them how they're* not? I'm sure the clearly intelligent look on my face gave Phillip every indication that I was getting this. But, just as a precautionary measure, he went on.

"So, if you know you can run a smaller sail on the inner forestay for a storm, you also know you have a backup sail you can run if, say, there is no storm, but your main headsail, the Genny, goes out. If the Genny rips or goes overboard, or something on it breaks, your 'storm sail,'" —he actually made the little hand quotation marks in the air— "can then act as your 'Genny,'" with the quotation marks again and a stern look to see if I really was getting this. I swear I heard some gears inside my brain groan to life and could feel a little rust fall to the bottom of my brain shop floor. Things were turning. If you know the properties of the system—in this case, that it runs from the mast to the deck and can hold a smaller sail—you can use it for an arguably unintended purpose. That really did make sense. *Absorbent and adhesive-backed*, I thought. That was the first "system" that came to my mind, and the minute it did, gears cranked into life, roaring, spinning and churning and taking me back to the side of the interstate, a long stretch of I-40 somewhere in Louisiana, standing next to my dad's big, black Peterbilt beauty where he first taught me this "creative systemizing" approach.

Having spent his eight seconds of fame as a bull rider, my dad transitioned, as many a cowboy does, to a thriving career as a big-rig, cattle-truck driver. My parents had long since divorced by then, well before I ever formed my first memory, and the entire time John and I were growing up, they occupied different parts of the nation—mom in New Mexico and dad in Alabama. When summers rolled around, my dad would line up a long-haul out to New Mexico, seventeen hours total, to come pick John and me up to bring us back with him to Alabama for the summer. He drove an enormous, shiny, black Peterbilt, the kind with the naked lady arched back on the mud flaps and two tall chrome pipes standing up like horns on each side of the cab. That truck was a beauty. It was on my way back to that beautiful truck after one of our side-of-the-road, get-out-and-do-your-business stops that I found myself in need of some good ol' daddy-doctoring.

While stumbling back, pulling and fidgeting with my little kid, elastic-waisted jeans, I managed to step on a hornet's nest or buried beehive or something, because a pack of monstrous, vicious, alien-like insects swarmed around me on the way back. I was running and flailing and swatting them with the toilet paper roll that was still clenched in my little fist. I had just about cleared them when I felt something on my eye. Out of instinct, I reached up and smacked at it. That must have smashed the wasp or bee or hornet stinger right into my lid, because I

could feel instantly the venom (or whatever putrid, seething substance those alien insects were carrying) burn into my skin. My eyelid puffed up immediately, and I was bawling at the top of my lungs by the time I got back to the Peterbilt, a tattered trail of toilet paper straggling behind me. My dad did a quick assessment, shifting my face left to right in his big calloused hand. He concluded the inspection with "Awww ... hell" and turned around to rummage through the passenger floorboard of the truck's cab, which was about at his eye level.

Much like his own daddy, my dad was a long-time Copenhagen connoisseur. He always had a big hunk of chaw packed down between his gums and lower lip. I came to love the smell of it as I associated Copenhagen with my dad and found myself strangely attracted to some pretty hideous redneck deadbeats in college because of it. But, unlike most, I know that tobacco is more than a sticky, cancer-causing, sickening habit. It can work wonders when you've been stung by alien wasps. My dad hooked his finger in his mouth and pulled the big wad of tobacco out from his bottom lip and slapped that sticky mess on my eye. As soon as he did, I swear I could feel wasp juice leaving my body. The tobacco wad was cool and wet and incredibly soothing. And, I even liked the smell. I'm sure I was smiling from the instant relief, caring none about the stray tobacco juice that was streaking down my face, coming perilously close to my mouth. *My dad had fixed it!*

He held the wad to my head while he kept rummaging around the floor of the cab for something to keep the tobacco on my face and contain the mess. And, as it seemed he always did, my dad found the perfect thing—a big, thick Maxi Pad, with wings. Don't ask me why my dad had a Maxi Pad in the cab of his truck. I'm sure he had many a lady friend join him on a haul or two, and perhaps she had left some remnants of her womanhood behind. Or perhaps he kept a pack of them around for some highly useful Peterbilt purpose—to contain a small oil spill, or patch a leak perhaps. I have no idea, but I was grateful that day that he did. I'm sure my dad thought twice about sticking a woman's period pad to my face, knowing full well what it was, but he didn't hesitate for long. One hand still pressed against my eye, he pulled the adhesive backing off with his teeth and slapped that pad right across my face, one wing crossing the bridge of my nose and the other reaching up to the corner of my scalp. My brother still likes to remind me how stupid I looked cruising the next 100 miles with a women's menstrual device slapped to my face and sticky, stinky tobacco juice crusted up from my eye all the way down to a black pool on the front of my t-shirt, but I didn't care—all my problems were solved.

An arguably unintended purpose, I thought. *Please!* In addition to the Maxi Pad, I'd seen my dad make a fishing line out of bailing twine, a perfectly good swing out of rope and a feed sack, and a lassoing dummy out of a bale of hay and some long horns. He could make anything out of anything, and I figured I could do the same. Show me how those lines and halyards and stays worked, and I could rig up a damn three-ring circus act on the boat that would make Barnum jealous. I also knew chaw could not only serve as a pleasurable pastime, assuming we wanted to bring a spittoon with us on the boat and take to spitting, but that we could also use it to draw out venom in case one of us was stung by a bee, hornet, or alien wasp. *So, creative systemizing? Check. What's next?*

Everything, that's what. All the lines and crap on the boat, they're all important, but they each had their own special names, none of which made sense to me. Unless I learned them all, I'd be the one out there shouting, "No the purplish rope on the left, that's wrapped around the silver ma-bob." I was not going to be the "silver ma-bob" gal. So, I made up a ton of stupid little rhymes and riddles to remind myself what things on the boat were. I remembered the furler because it will "curl her," as in curl the Genny up around the forestay. I knew "reefing" meant to bring the sails down because, if the opportunity presents itself, you never want to pass on a good time to "reef her." Get it? And I remembered the big steel drums that actually do all the heavy lifting on the boat are called winches. Why? Because, like beer wenches, they're big and hearty and do all the heavy lifting. Brilliant,

I know. Don't worry, my nautical dictionary will be coming out soon. But, I was starting to get it, somewhat. I, at least, wasn't referring to things quite as often as ma-bobs and doohickies and, God forbid, ropes, which is apparently the *worst* thing you can call something on a boat. It's so insulting. They're lines, get it? Not ropes.

Then Phillip started to talk about safety. *Safety? What's not safe about a boat?* He started walking me through man-overboard drills, which, I have to admit, did make sense. I mean, if you fell overboard, you would be kind of screwed. But don't fall overboard, and we won't have to run through the dangerous drill of coming to get your dumbass in the first place, am I right? So, I told myself, *Alright, ma-bob gal, don't fall overboard. What's next?*

"A fire," Phillip said. *Yeah, that sounds pretty bad too.* But I felt like he was kind of coming up with these wild, highly unlikely scenarios just to toy with me. *What's going to catch on fire?* I thought. Then I remembered the propane, the oven, the stove. *Doh!* So, we picked up some fire extinguishers and made ourselves practice the old P-A-S-S method—pull, aim, squeeze and sweep. I have to admit, the fire extinguishers were kind of fun. Phillip was pretty militaristic during these 'training days,' but I did get him to laugh a bit the first time I blew the extinguisher and it whipped around me like a wild fire hose. I was certainly laughing at him, ducking and running for cover. It took forever to get that magic poofy white stuff out of my hair. I'm not sure what I would have come up with to try and explain it to the guys back at the office. Phillip's lucky to have a shaved head. Why can't that be trendy for the ladies?

After the fire drills, we started researching first aid kits. "For longer voyages on vessels containing up to six people," Phillip read aloud from the product descriptions on the West Marine website, where everything costs twelve dollars more because it's the "marine" version. They're going to have to tell me some day what makes regular duct tape different from marine duct tape, other than the price. The first aid kits were a little pricey, too, and there were fifteen different ones to choose from—some for short trips or inland waters, some for coastal cruising and longer voyages, some with just the basic over-the-counter medications and wound care accessories and some with things like CPR equipment and "burn modules." I had no clue what "burn modules" were but I knew a thing or two about off-the-cuff wound care. Phillip's talk of bandages for cuts, burns, and scrapes took me back to Alabama, to Big Mom's carpeted, pink-and-paisley themed bathroom, water roaring into the tub and Big Mom telling me she was fixing to "doctor me up."

I had been riding with my dad that morning on his new roping horse, Rusty. My brother had hopped on the back so we were three-deep on Rusty and walking the gravel road from the pastures up to Big Mom's house. Now, I can't tell you what happened exactly. I barely remember the actual fall, but dad tells me the horse was stung by something. A hornet, probably, based on the whelp he found on the horse's hindquarter later, but, for whatever reason and without warning, Rusty reared back on his hind legs, his forelegs doing that classic Black Stallion-style bicycle kick, and he threw John right off the back. He then came stomping down, firmly planted his front legs and gave a massive buck with his rear, launching my dad and me up and over his head. Now, it was a good thing my dad held on to me when Rusty reared back, not such a good thing when he bucked us over his head and we slammed to the ground, me on the bottom and all two hundred and twenty pounds of my dad on top, and we proceeded to slide face-first across the gravel road.

My dad had a look of horror on his face when he rolled me over, pushed a blood-soaked swath of hair from my face, shook me to and asked, "Babes? Babes? You okay?" I tried to respond but couldn't, as I had a clot the size of Kansas in my mouth. I do remember that. Was it blood? Was it dirt? Was it blood-soaked dirt? I have no idea. All I know is the world started jostling around as he scooped me up and took off running toward the house, shouting for Big Mom. Big Mom had to be nearing sixty at the time, but she hoisted all of my sixty little pounds up close to her body and hauled my bloody carcass up every stair in the house, saying, in the calmest manner, as if she were looking at a rash on my arm, "Now, let's see what we got here." She took me to the bathroom and started drawing a bath, and I saw a couple bottles of hydrogen peroxide sitting on the edge of the tub. They're hard to miss, that old mud-brown bottle with the white cap. It was a home health product I was all too familiar with. Big Mom seemed to always have an endless supply of it and she broke it out anytime my brother or I had suffered a knick and needed to be "doctored up." That was the stuff that made a tiny little cut bubble and fizzle and burn like acid. That fuzzy white shit found cuts you never even knew you had. I knew what it was capable of and I watched Big Mom dump bottles of it into the tub.

Bottles! I started wriggling out of her grasp, protesting and wailing and begging for "anything but that!"

But Big Mom wasn't having it. Even my most fervent rebellion was not going to stop her from doing what she knew was right for me. With strength I had never imagined her capable of and not a single word, she plopped me in that vat of acid and every laceration on my body started fizzling and frothing until it looked like a bubble bath. I was flailing and sputtering and shrieking at her in protest, when she grabbed me by my bloody chin.

"Awww hush, it ain't that bad," she said. "Hell, I swish with it." And then she did the unthinkable. Big Mom tipped the bottle of hydrogen peroxide up and took a swig. I sat there dumbfounded, totally silent, only the soft sound of my fizzling skin floating between us, as she swished that foul stuff around in her mouth three or four times, her eyes locked tightly on mine. She then spit a white foamy mouthful out next to me in the tub and gave me a firm hmmpph look that shut me up entirely. I forgot completely that my skin was burning off, that I was in pain everywhere, or, even, that I had fallen and skidded across gravel. Clot? What clot? Big Mom just put hydrogen peroxide in her mouth! *Her mouth!* Could there *be* anything worse? And, just like that, I stopped complaining. I stopped crying, and I agreed with her. It really wasn't that bad.

See? A healthy perspective *and* a great lesson in wound care. Even at that age, and even while my skin was sizzling right off, I was tickled plumb pink just to be alive. And, while I already knew hydrogen peroxide worked well to clean fresh wounds, I now *also* knew it could

be used as an oral astringent. There wasn't anything on those piddly little first aid kit packages Phillip was reading that was going to teach me that. *Wound care. Done. What Captain wouldn't want me?* This was my internal, kickass country-self speaking, though. Outwardly, I knew I still had a ton to learn about sailing. Hell, I hadn't even actually done it yet. Hadn't even experienced it, much less actually *Did. It. Myself.* So, I continued my studies. I started to pick up a few basics about the mast, stays, and halyards, and the leech and luff of the sails. I had made up enough little riddles and rhymes (and stick diagrams) in my head to remember which side was port, which side starboard, and how to differentiate the bow from the stern. I was just starting to chip at the surface of sailing when Phillip found the first boat he wanted to take a look at. It had taken months for him to find one that was 'just right' enough to go check out, but when he did, he came home sporting that same little-kid-against-the-toy-store-window look he had when the sailing books came in. I swear that man, to be so serious and sophisticated, is really still a little boy at heart. He had printed out the listing, the specs from the manufacturer's website, reviews of the boat from sailing magazines and all sorts of other related web crap and had put it all neatly stapled and organized in a manila folder with a printed label and everything. I can't imagine he got much actual legal work done that day, amidst all of his boat dreaming. He was beyond cute. We made contact that evening and set up a "look-see" the following weekend.

Much like buying a house, there are often two brokers involved in a boat purchase, the boat seller's broker and the boat buyer's broker. If you find a boat you want to check out, usually you contact the seller's broker, line up an initial "look-see" (that's a technical term), walk through the boat, check it out and, if you like it, have your broker put in an offer to purchase it. Like a house, an offer to buy a boat is usually contingent on a satisfactory inspection and appraisal, known as a survey/sea-trial. This is where you hire an experienced surveyor to conduct an in-depth inspection of the boat to make sure there aren't any serious problems not visible to the naked (or inexperienced) buyer's eye. He also has the luxury during the survey/sea-trial to test systems that can't be tested without actually cranking the engine, turning all of those things on the panel off and on, or getting her out under sail. Having yet to line up our own broker, Phillip and I were broker-less, acting rogue at the time, scouring boat listings ourselves and setting up appointments on our own. Phillip contacted the seller's broker and set up a time for us to meet at the boat, step aboard and just get a good look at her. The seller's broker apparently had other intentions, though, when he tossed the lines, hollered into the wind and turned what was supposed to just be a look-see into my very first sail.

I remember fumbling through the pages of the American Sailing Association manual while Phillip drove us the forty-five minutes to where the boat was located, trying frantically to absorb everything at once and memorize all of these foreign terms, like leech and luff, beam reach and close haul. I figured if I *sounded* like I knew what I was talking about, they wouldn't know I really had no clue what I was doing, what I was supposed to be doing: how I should act, talk, even *sit* on a boat? It was my first time setting foot on a real, live sailboat. Excitement coursed through me like molten lava. I had to hold my elbows out like chicken wings while I read the manual to keep the flow from the air conditioning vents passing through my sweaty pits. Every time Phillip asked me a simple, two-word question like "You excited?" I would respond with gushing speeches, lengthy monologues conveying my every emotion and thought about boats, sails, yachtsmen and the sea. That's when he shoved the American Sailing Association safety manual in front of me. Smart move.

When we got there, we were greeted by the seller's broker, a ruddy, raucous man with a scar that traveled from the corner of his mouth up and around, almost to his nose, like a handlebar mustache. It could have been the product of him falling off a swing set when he was a kid, but I, of course, imagined that it had to have occurred when he was a grown man, full of grit and guile, and out on the open sea. It was probably a big fish hook that got caught in his mouth, and he yanked it out without flinching, slapped some bait on wound, bloody and wet, all while battling eight-foot seas and crashing waves—naturally. Anyone qualified to sell a sailboat must be this kind of character. Or so I thought.

I can tell you *now* exactly what kind of boat we were looking at— the make, the model, the design features, and the pros and cons—but that is now. *Then*, I only knew it was a thirty-four-foot sailboat, the make consisting of two words: some sea-related term followed by some intimidating adjective that conjured the image of a smashing hammer—something like "Sea Striker" or "Wave Crusher"—along those lines. At least that is how I had processed it at the time.

Phillip and I were new to this whole boat-buying enterprise, so we brought a ringer, a friend-of-a-friend-who-knew-a-guy who knew a lot about boats. And, boy did he. It seemed there wasn't anything on a boat this guy couldn't disassemble, diagnose, and fix with a pair of pliers and some wire. I was glad he was on our team. He was going to be our ace in the hole, our surveyor in disguise. But, Hook-Mouth picked up his scent immediately. After a few short exchanges and pointed questions, the broker could tell our "friend" was, in reality, one incredibly sharp sailor. He didn't seem bothered by it, though. Instead, the challenge invigorated him. He jumped right up into the cockpit, cranked the engine and said, "You just need to feel her under sail!" There was no offer on the table, no dollar figure had even been discussed, and this guy was willing to take us out on the open sea to show us what she could "really do." *Yes! We are going to the "sea."* I thought anytime you tossed the lines and headed out, you went to the sea. This was a free sail, and my *first*, to boot. There was no way we were turning that down. *Let's go!*

And go we did. We puttered out into a little harbor and everything was smooth and calm—a nice, peaceful, day sail. That's how it started at least, but it was soon to change. It was blowing a steady twenty knots that day, with gusts up to twenty-five. Hook-Mouth opted not to reef the sails and as soon as we made it out into the bay, with all the fetch, the wind found us. The boat heeled over instantly and the sails popped and pulled taut as the boat groaned to life. Luckily, I had found a good "nestle" spot port-side in the cockpit with my arms draped leisurely over the lifelines, merely for comfort. But when the boat kicked over, I gripped those puppies for dear life. We tilted over so far, I remember looking over my shoulder and watching everything tumble out of my jacket pocket and into the sea—a crumpled receipt, some lint, some change, and my favorite lipstick—all disappeared instantly, heading straight for the bottom. I was prepared to jump in right after my jettisoned belongings when the mast hit the water, which I thought would surely happen next.

Our ringer was steering the boat at the time and he shouted, "I'm buried to port!" I had no idea then what that meant, but I was sure it was important and I was sure it was not good. I thought about shouting it, too, to make sure Phillip and Hook-Mouth heard. "Hey, did you guys hear?! We're buried to port!" But I didn't say a word.

All of those cumbersome sailing terms had completely escaped me and were replaced only with expletives and things you shout while jumping out of an airplane. I looked down the port-side of the boat and saw the edge of the deck was underwater and then a silly sail term emerged on its own. *Rail, toe rail, that's our toe rail!* rang in my mind. *It's buried too!* Seeing how far we were heeled over, I had a pretty good feeling "buried to port" meant our ringer couldn't right us, not at the moment at least.

So, what did I do? Took a picture! Trust me, it was the best use of my useless sailing skills at the time. Document. Survive and document. That's about all I was good for. Thankfully, the boys proved to be incredibly sea-savvy. Our ringer held fast at the helm as Hook-

Mouth jumped up to the mast and began reefing the mainsail, casual as ever, laughing heartily, as he said, "I always say 'reef often, reef early'!" Phillip and I exchanged a look. *Yeah buddy, a little earlier next time.* But we weathered it out, got the sails down a bit and fell off the wind. I hadn't said a word since we'd nearly tipped over, mainly because I didn't know what *to* say. I was too excited to put any kind of coherent thought together. Much like the broker, I was hooked! As we motored back to the marina, it came out that the day's venture had been my first sail. The men looked at me with surprise and told stories of former girlfriends and significant others who, in the face of a similar experience, had either thrown up, cried, or demanded dry land immediately, thereby rightfully ensuring their place as "formers." I figured if the only thing I had lost that day was a tube of Revlon ColorStay, it was well worth it. I knew then and there that sailing was going to be, *had* to be, a big part of our future—the excitement of it, the momentum, the *adventure*. It was a desire screaming for fulfillment. While we didn't end up getting the "Gulf Pounder," or whatever I thought it was at the time, we did continue looking. We knew there was a boat out there for us. If we were going to travel the world, the Captain was going to need two solid, dependable ladies who thirsted for blue waters, lived to bury the rails and had no need for lipstick.

FOUR

93.46 Perfect

While looking back on it now I can easily say I had fun on my first sail. I mean it was exhilarating, a little frightening, and a little chilly—easily qualifiable as fun. But I know, now, that I wasn't really involved. I was just a spectator who clung to the lifelines and watched it all occur. Sure, that's always fun—when it's not your boat and not your responsibility. So, in that sense, I believe it's more accurate to say that I had not yet truly taken to sailing because I didn't yet *know* sailing. I hadn't held the lines in my own hands and felt the tension, the power. I didn't know what all was involved, how it all worked, what types of skills and characteristics made for a good sailor. And it would be some time before I came to really understand sailing and really enjoy it. I had no idea yet what it felt like to hear the boat groan and creak over six-foot waves in the black of night, to feel the fatigue in your arms from holding a heading for hours on end against unfavorable wind and waves, or to hear a crucial piece of equipment shatter overhead and watch a monstrous sail come fluttering down to the deck like a weeping flag. That would come. For now we just knew I hadn't gotten seasick yet, I was good at hanging onto the rails, and, so far, I had enjoyed it. This boat-buying business was still "a go."

The boat Hook-Mouth showed us was a 2001 Pacific Seacraft, an undeniably well-made quality blue water boat, but with an undeniably steep price. It was going to require some serious penny-pinching for us just to *get* that boat and another disheartening sum to get it in cruising condition. Unfortunately the Seacraft had been hit by lightning just a few months prior and all of the electronics had been zapped–think tens of thousands of dollars (easily) to replace all of that. It would have essentially cleaned us out for months. That would have required many more nights cooking red beans and rice at home rather than eating out. We definitely wanted a quality boat, but we also wanted (needed, really) a little leftover in the cruising kitty to maintain the boat and actually, you know, *cruise*. Our buddy, the Ringer, put us in touch with a local boat broker to help us scout out some other options. As often happens in the boating community, someone who is first introduced to you professionally–merely as a broker, rigger, or bottom-job guy–soon becomes a friend. Our broker was no different. Not only was Kevin an excellent broker, intuitive and patient, he was also like-minded. He could easily see how we wanted to use the boat and what kind of boat we needed to accomplish that goal. After a couple of weeks researching available listings, Kevin found us three prospects:

1. A 1990 34' Pacific Seacraft (same model as the Pacific Seacraft we had previously considered but ten years older and about half the price) located in St. Petersburg, FL;

2. A 1985 Hinterhoeller Niagara 35 (Canadian built, a model unknown to us, but one our broker repeatedly said he had a "really good feeling about") in Punta Gorda, FL; and

3. A 1989 Tayana 37 (a solid, proven blue water boat, like a "tank with sails," according to Kevin, and this one reportedly had "all the bells and whistles") in Daytona Beach, FL.

It was a pretty promising list. Each of the boats were the right build-quality and condition for the type of cruising we wanted to do and each had its own unique design features, add-ons, and upgrades that would provide the comfort, reliability, and agility we were looking for. It was clear Kevin had really listened and worked hard to find boats that would adequately suit our needs and fit our budget. It was weird looking at these boats on paper. One of them could be the one! *Our* boat. Our ticket to ocean travel. Our someday home. You hate to count your chickens, or mentally sail your prospects, before they ... you know. But it was too tempting not to! We decided to check out all three in one weekend. *Road Trip!*

A lot of people have asked me: "A sailboat? Really? Nights and days on end, stuck together on a tiny, little boat? Annie, are you sure?" I can tell you, my immediate answer is: "Of course, I'm sure." With Phillip, I'm always sure. I would climb into a crate with him and ride cargo across the Atlantic if he asked me to. But, if you're considering the idea—world travel with someone in a sailboat—I highly recommend, as a baby step, the Road Trip. One of the best ways to find out if you can spend hours cramped in a tiny space with someone without beginning to plot their slow, painful death is to jump in a car with the lucky lad and cover twelve hundred miles in one weekend. That will tell you real quick. After our many travels together, Phillip and I were quite certain we were prepared to step into any small vessel and spend exorbitant amounts of time together. However, this technically would be our first really long road trip and, I'm proud to say, despite the many miles we had to cover, we had a fantastic time together.

Our plan was to drive down on a Friday, stay the first night in St. Petersburg, check out the Pacific Seacraft in St. Pete on Saturday morning, and make the drive to Punta Gorda to check out the Niagara that afternoon. Then we would hightail it to a hotel in Daytona Beach to check out the Tayana on Sunday morning and make the six- to seven-hour drive home on Sunday afternoon. Three days. Three boats. Twelve hundred miles. Yeah, you better really like someone to make that trip together.

So, the Pacific Seacraft. We were looking at this one to compare it to the 2000 model we had taken out for my first sail a few weeks back. It must be true what they say—you always hold a bit of a soft spot for your first, that or a blissfully-skewed image at least—because if the 2000 Seacraft was akin to my hot, high school boyfriend, the 1990 was the pot-bellied, balding version of him at our twenty-year reunion. Just not the same spark. The 1990 also had not been well-maintained—hence the "hair loss" and "weight gain," and it was all dark wood below so it felt very confined and constricted, like you had stepped down into a dimly-lit wood-paneled hunting lodge. It wouldn't have surprised me at all to see some wild critter stuffed and mounted down below. And I, of course, can only tell you what I saw, smelled, felt, and thought at the time, which focused primarily on the general look and feel of the boat. "It was way too dark down there, Phillip, and that upholstery? Puke!" My observations had nothing to do with how the boat actually *sailed* or anything important like that. I just didn't really know enough about sailing at the time to know what was important, what could be changed or discarded if we didn't like it, what was permanent and, of particular importance, what features would hinder or help the performance and capability of the boat as a, you know, *sailing* vessel and all. Thankfully Phillip was there to worry about all of that, leaving me free to focus on layout and decor. Taking both of those aspects into consideration, we were interested in the 1990 Seacraft but certainly not enamored. We both walked away with a kind of well-that-was-one-option attitude, secretly hoping the Niagara would impress us a little more but wondering internally: *What if they just got worse?*

Forty-five minutes later, we proved that theory wrong. The Niagara was tugging playfully on her dock lines and smiling at us when we walked up–like a little puppy at the pound, wagging her tail and squealing, "Pick me! Pick me!" I don't know how else to explain it other than she just looked happier than the Seacraft.

In addition to the obvious happy quality, Canadian-built Hinterhoellers also have a reputation as solid, sea-worthy vessels. We were looking at a 1985 Niagara that was primarily a one-owner. The seller, Jack, had owned it since 1989 and you could just tell he loved that boat. He greeted us with a bright smile and big paw handshakes and jumped right on the boat with us to tinker around. The Niagara was extremely well-cared for–polished and clean, organized and tidy. Despite being the oldest boat we had looked at, she was easily in the

best condition. The Niagara was most definitely Jack's baby. And for good reason. Jack had sailed the boat several times in the Mackinac race from Lake Huron to Mackinac Island, MI, a 290-mile freshwater course, single-handedly. As a result, just about every system on the boat was streamlined and rigged for quick, easy, single-handed use. He knew every single system on the boat, in and out–every screw, every thru-hull, every wire, every nut, every bolt. Jack was like a walking interactive owner's manual for the Niagara. And, while he had raced her some, Jack and his wife, Barb, primarily used the boat for cruising. From quick weekend trips to months down in the Keys, they had put a lot of blue water miles on that boat so she was set up perfectly for cruising. But Jack and Barb were now retired and, as tough as it was for them to give it up, after decades of wonderful sails on the boat, they were ready to retire from cruising as well. Jack told us it had taken them a long time to finally decide to sell the boat and they wanted to make sure she fell into good hands. *These are good!* I wanted to say, with my hands stretched out toward them, palms up. *They are. I promise. Put her here!* Phillip and I had both already developed a pretty hearty craving for their boat.

The Niagara had a spacious cockpit with plenty of room to kick back and stretch out at the helm. Phillip told me time and again that the cockpit of the boat is like your living room, the "room" that you're going to spend the most time in. "It has to be comfortable," he would say. A couple of the boats Phillip had looked at when he started shopping had a "T" cutout in the cockpit to accommodate a massive steering wheel. Meaning, you couldn't stretch out in the cockpit. It's

like trying to sleep on a loveseat. You've either got to bend your knees or hang a foot off. The other cockpits we had seen felt like the stuffy, formal "sitting" room at the front of the house, with rigid high-back chairs and doilies, much more for *show* than comfort. But this one, on the Niagara, felt like the comfy den in the back with the old, grungy couches where everyone piles in on Saturdays to watch the game. It was just so damn comfortable.

We felt the same about the galley and saloon down below. And, I'm sorry, but every time I see the word saloon, I can't help but picture one of the old whiskey-busting joints with the double-swinging doors you see in old westerns. Makes me want to put on an old bouffant dress and drink bourbon. But that's just me. And it doesn't take much to make me want to do that anyway.

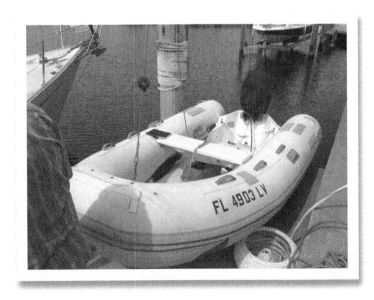

The Niagara also came with a hard-bottom dinghy and a fifteen horse-power, two-stroke outboard–a rare find and one our broker Kevin mentioned four or five times at least. "Did you see the dinghy?" he asked. He was really excited about the dinghy. But so were we! We tried to put on business-appropriate faces, showing some interest but not too much interest. We told Jack, Barbara, and their broker that while we had some other boats to look at, we were definitely impressed with the Niagara, its exceptional condition an obvious reflection of Jack's meticulous maintenance of it, and that we would be in touch. But as soon as Phillip and I turned our backs and started walking toward the car, the desire for that boat was already pumping through us. Phillip had told me: "You just know when you step on the boat." And we both knew. The Niagara was right–the layout, design, and decor all met my approval and Phillip okay'ed all of the important sailing stuff. We both flirted with the idea: this boat could be the one.

The Niagara was all we could talk about on the way to Daytona Beach. Looking back on it, it's probably a good thing no one else made that trip with us, because they probably would have jumped right out of the car and hitchhiked home. Our imaginations swelled with images of the two of us, our hands gently laid on the wheel while the Niagara glided through crystal green waters. I would have doodled the name *Niagara* with little hearts and stars around it all during the drive home in a spiral-bound notebook in my Trapper Keeper if I, you know, had a Trapper Keeper. That boat was all we could think about. While we still had one more boat to check out on this trip–Tayana the tank, a beast of a boat–we both had a sneaking feeling we had already found ours.

Tayanas are Taiwanese-built boats, hand-crafted inside, so each one is unique, with a reputation of being sturdy as hell, built to survive the apocalypse. This one certainly met that mark. Her size and stature were definitely impressive but the remainder I would have to describe only as interesting. Kind of like when your best friend tells you your blind date for the evening is not smoking hot but, rather, "really interesting." It doesn't bode well. And let's just hope you weren't described to him as someone whose "size and stature are definitely impressive." The couple who owned the Tayana were in their late sixties, had been living aboard and cruising it for about ten years, and they were ready to sell the boat and settle down on dry land. While they were super nice, they just didn't seem to have the same cruising needs as Phillip and me, so the boat wasn't rigged out the way we would do it.

Now I know everyone rigs a boat to their liking–upgrading or modifying certain things so they perform and function just the way *they* want them to. But, for whatever reason, while all of Jack's modifications on the Niagara seemed to suit us, the modifications made on the Tayana seemed to hinder use of the boat in the way we intended. For example: the helm. *My God.* That thing had more instruments and gadgets on it than a NASA spacecraft. I'll bet you could launch a nuclear warhead from it if you crossed a wire or two. You couldn't even really see beyond it to look out on the waves or water, to get a good visual of the horizon. And I didn't even know at the time how really important that is, but somehow a feeling of claustrophobia just came over me when I sat behind that wheel. *Get me out of here!*

Another problem area was the nav station. There were panels upon panels of buttons, levers, toggles, etc. It looked like you could perform laser surgery right there on the boat. The seller was also left-handed, but the nav station was starboard, so he had rigged a special pullout slat for his elbow so he could write left-handed. He had also installed a swivel stool for the nav station because it had no seat. And, the nav station was all the way forward almost to the v-berth—definitely not ideal if you're in the cockpit and need to get quickly to the radio or electronics or your charts. All of this told us it wasn't right. The Tayana just wasn't right, but the real okay-that-does-it moment came just as we were leaving.

Before we stepped off the boat and bid the nice couple adieu, Phillip started looking around the cockpit a bit, craning his neck here and there around the massive instrument panel on the helm. The owner asked him what he was looking for. "The swim ladder," Phillip responded, and both the husband and wife immediately started shaking their heads. "Oh, we don't swim," they said. And *that* really sealed the deal for us. The Tayana was a sturdy, well-built boat, but this one just wasn't set up for cruisers like us. *Cruisers who don't swim.* I couldn't really wrap my head around it. That's like cheerleaders who don't smile. It's just not right. One of the most important aspects of sailing, for us, would definitely be the water—being able to see it and swim in it. While we could add a swim ladder, sure, and make all sorts of other modifications, the boat just really wasn't set up or laid out to be "cruise-ready" for us. As Phillip and I walked away from the Tayana, we both knew. Out of the three boats we had checked out that weekend, the Niagara easily took the gold. I felt sorry for the Tayana, anyway, having to follow the Niagara. She didn't stand a chance.

We got Kevin on the phone on our way home and told him our thoughts on the Niagara. Kevin was stoked. "It was the dinghy, wasn't it?" he asked playfully. *Sure, it was the dinghy. And every other freaking thing on that boat!* Like I said, the cockpit was perfect–roomy, clean not cluttered, and would allow both of us to lay down on either side and look out on the horizon. Also, now that I had seen a boat or three, I was starting to get a better base to draw from and I could tell that, down below, the Niagara felt much bigger than the other boats we had been on, although it actually wasn't. It was the layout, with all of the appliances, cabinetry and seating pushed out along the exterior, leaving a large open area in the middle to walk around in.

Other layouts had the galley sink or other counter jutting out in the middle of the living area, slicing it up. When you stepped down

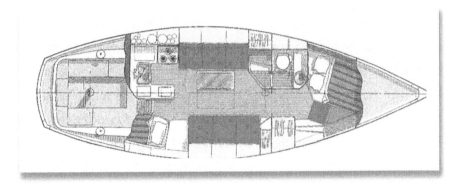

below, you immediately imagined yourself sucking, in and saying, "Excuse me," while you squeezed around the jut-out to let someone by. They just felt tiny. The Niagara was big, breezy, open. "But with lots of grips," Phillip told me, as he walked through, grabbing a built-in hand-rail about eye-level on the starboard side. *Okay, yeah, good grips,* I thought, dismissing him a bit. *Whatever. This place is awesome!*

The Niagara also had a separate, stand-up shower stall, as opposed to the sit-and-spray set-up of some of the other boats where the shower head was simply rigged right over the toilet. It also had a water heater. Even I, the cruising rookie, could appreciate that. The Niagara was hitting home runs left and right for me. But, like I said, that was just layout and decor. On the sailing front, it seemed the Niagara was hitting all of the high notes for Phillip too. It was a sloop rig with all lines run back to the cockpit for easy single-handed sailing. The genoa–the powerhouse sail on the front–was fairly new (2006) and Jack had added lazy jacks to the mainsail to make lowering it easier. Niagaras also had a reputation as durable sea vessels, blue water yachts they call them, because they can cross the "blue waters" of the ocean, take you all over the world, pretty much, and bring you back in one piece. Overall, she was a hell of a boat. The only thing that gave Phillip pause was the mast height–fifty feet–and the draft–five foot, two inches. She was tall and deep. The very qualities that made her an all-star at sea also made her a bit harder to sail into little shallow inlets and bayous along the coast. The mast height was going to prevent us from getting under a good number of bridges in our local waters around Pensacola and from traveling certain portions of the Intracoastal Waterway entirely. The keel depth was also going to limit us from getting into some shallow anchorages.

But this was a recurring theme. One of the things that became an unavoidable yet repetitive nuisance when we were boat shopping was the never-ending trade-off. *You mean I can't take all of the features that I love and want in a boat and mash them together to make the perfect boat?* Sorry, my friend. In the boat business, it seems it's always give and take. In order to have a boat that can travel oceans, you've got to give up a little agility and maneuverability to have a heavier, sturdier boat. If you want a boat that can go anywhere in the ICW, you've got to give up some mast height and a deeper keel, which also means you're giving up some of the boat's steadiness–her sure-footedness if you will–at sea. Always, it's this for that. Like a savvy bargain shopper at the flea market, you're constantly bartering. "I'll give you a quarter for the orange-haired troll doll if you'll throw in that doily." "What, no doily? Alright, a dime for the doll."

But, the Niagara met about 93.46% of our needs. She was beautiful–classic lines with just the right amount of wood trim, spacious interior and proven capability at sea. She was also incredibly well-maintained. Barbara and Jack had taken exceptional care of her and we were eager to fall into their footsteps and take good care of her ourselves. It was decided.

"Yep. Agreed, Kevin. Put in an offer," Phillip said through a smile.

An offer. This was it. We were setting everything in motion. If accepted, the offer would lead to a survey/sea-trial which, with Jack as the primary caretaker, we were secretly confident would only reveal more awesome things about the boat and its exceptional condition. Surely. Then the boat would be ours! *Our boat. Sigh.* Phillip and I made the long drive home in a hazy dream-state. We were really doing it. Putting in an offer. On a boat. And not just any boat, a sailboat–a 93.46% perfect sailboat.

FIVE

Survey(or) Says...

He clambered up to us that morning, pot-bellied and boisterous, lugging a large, seemingly vintage toolbox of sorts, a satchel and a rolling briefcase. Sweat was already beading up around his hairline. Even the smallest of tasks, like opening the latch to his case, seemed to require small grunts and more sweat. He extended a wet, meaty paw to each of us, introducing himself only as Kip. No last name. Just Kip. Two silver, pirate-like loops hung from each of his earlobes and a gaudy, over-sized gold ring hung heavily on his left hand. I would have never taken him for the surveyor had he not handed us each a card when he walked up. It too, though, only read "Kip." Like he was more famous than Madonna.

We were back in Punta Gorda, this time with our broker Kevin in tow, for the survey sea/trial. Much like when you buy a house, our offer on the boat was contingent upon a satisfactory survey/sea trial. It was our chance to look under the hood, so to speak, and make sure all of the systems on the boat were in working order before we paid a good chunk of change for her. The survey is meant to uncover potential

problems with the boat that you perhaps cannot see or test upon gross inspection—like issues with the hull or engine or the electronics, for example, or things you could not uncover when you first looked at the boat because you either: (a) couldn't access or test them, or (b) wouldn't know how to test them even if you could. Cue Kip, the savvy surveyor we hired at Kevin's recommendation and the man with the mission—find anything that might qualify as a potential problem with the boat. In order to do the survey, they had to do a "haul-out," which is just about as technical as it sounds. They hauled the boat out of the water so we all could have a look at her underwater parts.

Our boat came out glistening and dripping, fin keel and all, and my first thought was: *She's huge!* I mean that as a compliment because you forget, when half of her is hidden under the water, how really big she is down there–like a glacier, or Kim Kardashian. I had no idea at the time how important it is to have so much counter-weight under the water to counteract the power of the sails, but it made sense. The keel is like her weeble-wobble component–ensuring no matter how much she "wobbles," she won't tip over. I would learn all of that later, when we found ourselves heeled over to the tune of about thirty degrees when we were sailing the boat back from Punta Gorda, but I only knew at the time that she was huge! At our broker's direction, we had hired colorful Kip who, despite the eccentric exterior, had a reputation for being one of the most highly-rated surveyors in the area. Our boat was hanging there in straps, her underside exposed for all the world to see. She certainly wasn't shy and, apparently, neither was Kip. He immediately began digging around and rattling through his things and getting to work on her. Phillip and I stood in bewilderment as Kip pulled out tools and began beating the bottom of the boat with a yellow hammer and shouted, to no one in particular, "Every gal loves a good bangin' in the morning!"

Kevin assured us Kip had a reputation for being extremely thorough and brutally honest, which is just what we wanted. If there was anything wrong with the boat, we wanted Kip to find it and give us the run-down. And, find it he did. At each point Kip accosted the hull of the boat with his yellow hammer we heard a high-pitched ringing "whack." It appeared this noise pleased Kip as he would continue along unphased by each shrill note, until he reached the area where the strut is fastened to the hull. When Kip struck near this area we all heard a dull, sickening thud, much *un*like the shrill, high-pitched sounds that had preceded it. Kip immediately stopped, struck the area again. Another deep, low thud. He struck the area to the left and right of it. High-pitched shrieks. He struck the area again. *Thud.* Kip started writing feverishly on his clipboard, and he circled the area with his hammer while we frowned. Like when you're laid back on the couch, telling your psychiatrist about the dream you had where you captured kittens and ate them and she starts scribbling furiously on her pad, we all wondered: *What are you writing there, Kip? What does that mean?*

We all came around a bit disheartened and examined the spot Kip had whacked and circled. Kip explained that it seemed there had been some water intrusion in the hull and there was a small pocket of water above the propeller shaft on the starboard side. Thankfully Kevin was there. This is where it really pays to have solid boating "counsel"

on board when you're thinking about buying a boat. Kevin got his best "bottom-job" guy on the phone–"Bottom-Job Brandon" who would later become another one of our trusted and valued boating friends–and got an estimate for a potential repair.

Brandon was able to give us a rough estimate of $2,500 to repair the ominous "thud," which didn't give us too much heartburn and it certainly wasn't a deal-breaker. To be honest, it was going to take something pretty radical to qualify as a deal-breaker for us. We were quite smitten with that boat. The owner, Jack, came around to investigate as well and seemed equally surprised by the water intrusion. He assured us he had not noticed it when the boat had been hauled out in July of the previous year, which also gave us comfort. We determined later the fact that we had hit that speed bump early on actually turned out to be a good thing because it seemed the sting of it was quickly forgotten once we got out on the water and into the wind. The rest of Kip's bangin' on the hull proved the Niagara's nether parts were in top-notch condition. Our gal had a very impressive bottom you might say. Kip even told Jack himself what great shape the boat was in given her age–a hearty twenty-eight years. With the survey portion done, they dropped her back in the water so we could continue with the sea-trial.

It was a beautiful day–not a cloud in the sky and just the right amount of wind. We hoisted the sails and felt her take off. And while I had already been indoctrinated *somewhat* into the sailing experience when we took the Pacific Seacraft out for my first sail, this was vastly different. Jack handled the boat like a true expert–probably because he is the expert when it comes to that boat. When Jack unfurled the headsail, the genoa, whom we now call "Genny" because, trust me, she is a she–powerful and persuasive–the boat heeled gently to port. Rather than the pop, groan and near tip-over I suffered the last time the wind found our sails, this was a smooth, pleasant experience. I experienced the same sense of awe as I did when I saw the keel for the first time. The genoa was massive too. She stretched from the bow all the way back to the mast and beyond. Curled coyly away on the forestay, I just had no idea she was so big. It was like a Phoenix rising for the first time and spreading its giant wings before you. Even being a novice sailor, I could tell she was the real powerhouse. Genny. The sail with the truly adventurous spirit. "You want to go?" she asked me playfully. "Follow me. I'll take you there."

Kip continued to tinker around the boat, flipping switches, checking systems, testing things and each time returning to us with smiles and thumbs up. Jack trimmed the sails with ease and the boat moved forward effortlessly. I had no knowledge of the wind direction–whether we were going upwind or downwind, were on a broad reach or close haul–I just knew the boat was moving, by power of the sails alone, and that it was beautiful. I didn't know at the time that this sail would be followed by hundreds of countless others. Some, just as beautiful and breathtaking, others scary and heartbreaking, but I will always remember that first one and how awe-stricken I was at the sight of the Genny alone. It was our first time sailing on the Niagara.

We all came back to the marina on a bit of a "sail high." Kevin was smiling at us. We were smiling at each other. Even Kip couldn't help but hide a grin. He packed up his bags and satchel back at the dock

and told us he'd write us up a "real good report." Aside from the small issue with the hull, the boat had passed Kip's rigorous test with flying colors. Kevin also took us aside and told us how impressed he was with how the boat handled, how easy it was to sail and how quick! Kevin felt confident this boat was a really good fit for us. Phillip and I shook hands with Jack and Barbara and told them we'd be in touch, each of us feeling as though the day had gone well and the boat would soon be under new owners. For Jack and Barbara it seemed bitter-sweet. While they appeared to like us and felt the boat was going to a good home with Phillip and me, they were also sad to see her go. They had sailed and cruised and enjoyed that boat for more than twenty years. That's a long time to love a thing. And a boat is not an easy thing to let go. But Barbara and Jack hugged us warmly and waved back heartily as they left the marina to head home.

Giddy from the day's sail and the success of the survey, we decided to take Kevin out on the town for a big steak dinner and an even bigger red wine. The conversation began, naturally, with the boat—all the things we wanted to do to it, the places we wanted to go in it. Basically, it. Us on it. Us storing it. Us sailing it. Us cruising it, and everything that entailed. But, as the wine kept coming, the conversation turned more toward us—Kevin, Phillip and me—our past, our experiences, big adventures, embarrassing moments, good, you know, *stories*. Okay, I was clearly steering the conversation. Those boys would sit around and talk about battery chargers and heat-shrink wires for days if I let them. They needed my help. Somehow I was able to steer us toward talk of the past and how I had been a cheerleader in high school.

If I recall there was someone who walked by in a full-length knee brace, crotch-to-ankle with straps and Velcro. I started laughing a bit to myself because I remembered having to wear one of those once. I was waiting tables at the time. Yes, still with the brace on. My little Ford Escort wasn't going to pay for itself. But, it drove me crazy that the brace always slid down. The bottom would slip down to the top of your shoes like pant legs, moving the one movable "joint" part in the brace down below your knee so you could no longer bend at the knee. It was really bothersome. So, I was telling the boys how, when I had to wear mine, I had fashioned some homemade suspenders for it out of bungee cords—ironically the very kind we use on the boat to lash down all sorts of things now. See? I was honing my boat skills well before I ever set foot on a boat.

Anyway, while the suspenders were entertaining enough, the instant joke was made about how I could put a lot of pins, clips and other insignia on them–sport some real flare, like I was waiting at T.G.I.Fridays, except it was Kripple Creek in Clovis, New Mexico. True story. So, the brace lead to the knee, the knee had been injured, the ACL had been busted and "How?" was answered with an "Oh, in high school. I was a cheerleader in high school." *How quickly we transition.* Then memories of my cheerleading days sunk in, and I knew I had to treat the boys to one in particular. I actually let them believe they were going to get some steamy story about me and my co-captain Bobby, a girl, and a hot little Latino one at that, when we were alone one night in the locker room. *I know, I'm terrible.* But instead they got this. It's way better, and 93.46% true.

We were cheering at a basketball game the night the pom-pom incident occurred–nothing incredibly eventful really, just some hum-drum Tuesday night game–us, the Wildcats, versus them, whomever. I was in the thick of it, starting chants, watching our lines, popping my arms vigorously in the classic cheer motions: the infamous "V" for victory and the exceedingly effective "power punch" move–one fist planted firmly on the hip and the other punched straight up to the sky. *Pow!* That one guarantees a win every time. I looked down the line to make sure the girls were on beat and hitting their marks, completely oblivious to what was happening on the court, when I was slammed hard by a player who had leapt off the court to try and save a ball from going out of bounds. The impact itself, while somewhat similar to a full-frontal collision with a Mac truck, actually wasn't too bad, but it knocked me back about three feet, where I slammed onto my ass, and scooted the rest of the way to the brick wall of the gymnasium, hitting that with a royal thud. While the blow wasn't bad, what it caused me to do was every bit of bad, mortifying actually.

I peed.

I couldn't help it. My "hold-it" mechanism was in shock and once the floodgate cracked the slightest bit open, I couldn't stop it. I emptied my entire bladder beneath my flailed-out skirt on the gym floor. Thankfully, Bobby made it to me first. She was my co-captain, my best friend and just the kind of scrappy advocate I needed at that moment–like the "Fixer" for the mafia. As she neared me and I felt the rest of the onlookers swooping in, I grabbed a fistful of her cheer top, pulled her in close and disclosed to her my sad state of affairs. "I just peed my pants." And, I know I wasn't wearing *pants, per se,* but that's what you say, isn't it? I mean, when someone makes you laugh to the point of squirting, you don't say, "Stop. Stop it. I'm going to pee my skirt." No, it's your pants. You're going to pee your *pants.* No matter what you're wearing–pants, shorts, a cheerleading skirt, even those hideous gaucho capris–it's peeage through pants. And I had most certainly done it. I'm sure Bobby did a little too when I told her. But her laughter stopped immediately when she accidentally placed a hand squarely in the outskirts of my puddle and the gravity of my situation sunk in. *I* was the only thing covering my incriminating spill.

"The pom-poms," Bobby said, and I gave her a smug look. *Who gives a fuck about the pom-poms? I'm swimming in a puddle of my own bodily fluid.* "Scooch back against them and we'll use them to hide the … Your …" Bobby didn't know what really to call it. *What, my puddle? My own little golden pond?* That's what it was. But, she had a brilliant idea. The pom-poms were right behind me, a big, fluffy pile of them. I smushed up against them and pretended to lean into them to rise while carefully molding them around the spillage underneath me. As I stood, the crowd began to rise with me and clap–a sort of "injury ovation" if you will. Bobby and I hobbled out the back door of the gym to the girls bathroom where we crumpled to the floor and peed some more. What did it matter then? I was already soaked.

It wasn't long, though, before we heard the girls on the line start up a new chant. A good one too. One of my favorites: "We Are Number One." It's got a nice little ditty in the second verse with a fun hip swivel–real sexy cheerleading stuff–and, you get to use the … The thought hit Bobby at the same time. *The pom-poms.* That cheer required the pom-poms. Of course. Out of all the damn chants we have, and the stupid JV girls pick one of the few that requires pom-poms. Bobby and I scrambled out of the bathroom, slid the gym door open a crack and peeked our heads in. It was a miracle. Somehow my puddle had gone unnoticed. Whatever cheap, Chinese plastic-equivalent they use to make pom-poms—a cousin to the polyester in our cheer skirts, I imagine—was marvelously absorbent because there wasn't a drop left of my pee on the floor. There were however, drops flying! With every vigorous pop of the pom-pom by the girls, a nice little smattering of drops would shake out and rain down to the floor. Some of the girls began to eye their pom-poms oddly, watching the little mist that jumped out of them every time the beat hit. Some even used a pause in the chant to make a quick wipe of the mist from their arms and faces. My pee, which I had once bore alone in a sopping puddle beneath me, had now been effectively disseminated amongst the entire squad. Distribute the load, I guess, and no one really carries the burden—real team spirit stuff. And, by the end of it, the girls had done a pretty damn fine job of drying out those pom-poms, saved Bobby and I the trouble of having to do it later, at least.

Okay, so it wasn't battery chargers and MPT controllers, but Phillip and Kevin laughed so hard I'm pretty sure they peed a little too. That got Phillip to thinking about the head on the boat, though, then the capacity of the holding tank and talk soon shifted back to the boat—boat parts, boat systems, more boring boat crap. I told myself the pom-pom detour had been fun, at least, while it lasted. It was pretty exciting, though, to know we were now talking about *our* boat, pretty much anyway. The offer on the Niagara was contingent on the survey/ sea trial, but Kip had given us every indication his report was going to be stellar. Everything else was just a matter of paperwork–signing documents, getting insurance, etc. After that, the boat was just sitting in Punta Gorda, waiting on us.

SIX

You Mean, You and I, We?

"So, when are they going to bring the boat to us?" I asked sweetly. Phillip and I were curled up on the couch, feasting on a fat pork chop he had made for dinner. Phillip stopped chewing for a minute and looked at me earnestly. I kept chewing and stared back at him. Blinking like a gentle deer in the meadow. *What?* my expression said. Blink. Blink. Smile. Phillip put his fork down, set his plate on the end table and turned to me. It looked like he was going to tell me I had some form of incurable cancer or something. "What?" I said out loud this time.

"Sweetheart," he said slowly. "They're not going to bring it to us."

They're not, I thought. *What? Why?*

Phillip was still staring sternly at me. "Annie, honey, we have to go get it," he told me. His eyes looking back and forth at mine, first my right, then my left, then back to my right again, as if he was *really* hoping I would get this. "We have to sail her home."

"You mean, you and I, we? *Us?*" I asked him.

"Well," Phillip said, looking a little skeptical about the whole thing. "So far."

This was the night we bought the boat. The 'buying' part was actually pretty uneventful. After the success of the survey, it was a pretty quick process after that. A slight move by Jack–to account for the hull issue discovered during the survey–another slight move by us and we easily found comfortable middle ground. We made the final offer, which Jack and Barbara accepted, and that glistening Niagara was then ours. Ours, in Punta Gorda, though–a whole Gulf of Mexico away.

"Oh," I said a little surprised, but immediately shifted. "Well, that's even better. Boat Trip!!" I sang it in the same commercial jingle manner as I had "Road Trip!" when Phillip told me we would be traveling to three cities to see three boats in one weekend. *This was going to be awesome!*

Phillip just picked up his glass of wine and took another sip, eyeing me quietly. I don't think he wanted to spring the grave news on me that night, while we were toasting and celebrating the boat purchase. *Best to wait*, I'm sure he thought. He raised his glass with a half smile and said, "Yeah. Okay. A *boat* trip."

But I soon learned by "trip" Phillip meant a full-on Gulf of Mexico crossing in our new boat. We were going to drive down to Punta Gorda and sail that boat back to Pensacola. A boat that was new to us, a passage that was new to us and with one mate who was new to sailing entirely. We were going to take all of that "newness" and sail it right off the coast of Florida, over one hundred miles offshore and hope we made it back to Pensacola in one piece. That's what he meant by "trip." While the seriousness of the trip *started* to sink in over the course of the next few weeks when we started planning and purchasing piles of safety equipment, I have to say, it really still didn't. Even as I was standing there, looking at all of the flares, flashlights, emergency foods, life jackets, jacklines, an EPIRB, dozens of maps, more flares and fire extinguishers, I couldn't imagine a scenario where we would actually need all of this stuff. I mean, I knew what we were doing could be dangerous. Sure, something could happen to the boat, we could be stranded out there, but I just figured the same was true when you step on a cruise ship, right? And, it was highly unlikely the boat would actually sink, right? Or that if we did find ourselves in trouble that we wouldn't be able to radio in, call the Coast Guard, something, right? *Not always,* Phillip was trying to convey to me. He was patient, but I just wasn't getting it. He kept drilling me on fire safety, use of the EPIRB, the location of the ditch bag, man over-board drills, on and on. *Why was he sucking the absolute fun out of everything?* I was trying. I really was, but I was naive and he was rightfully frustrated with me. One final snap at me and I shut down. *Okay, fine. I get it. I have no idea what I'm doing. I'm going to crash the boat, lose the EPIRB and fuck it all up.* I was starting to doubt myself–not my stamina, my durability, but perhaps my ability to respond correctly if, on the off chance, we *did* find ourselves in a situation that required *all* of that safety crap and more. I was worried about that–pulling the pin on the fire extinguisher before trying to use it, remembering to grab the ditch bag before ditching the boat. But, I just wasn't *scared.* Not yet, at least, and I didn't know that I ever would be, until I got out there. I needed to just get out there.

I'm a pretty rough-and-tumble kind of gal. I figured I could weather the majority of the wet, uncomfortable, tiring hours, but surely there would be some fun involved–some beautiful, glorious, sun-drenched moments on the deck, my hair blowing in the wind. *That was going to happen at least once, right?* Well, it could and it couldn't. I simply had no idea at the time how volatile sailing could really be. The fact that it is completely, and I mean utterly and inescapably, dependent on the weather. No wind means no sailing. Extreme wind means extremely rough sailing. Bad weather means bad sailing. Wet weather means wet sailing, and so on. On and on. And, while sailing can, at times, be just what I envisioned, a pristine sunny day, the wind dancing through your hair while you lay, stretched out like a Brazilian supermodel on the deck. *I don't know about you, but I always look like a supermodel in my daydreams, and Brazilian–always.* The remaining 68.43% of the time, though, it's work. Hard, manual labor. Up and down the companionway stairs, holding the helm against rolling waves, cleaning, scrubbing, cooking, adjusting the sails, coiling the lines, closing the hatches, opening the hatches, cleaning, scrubbing, cooking, folding, packing, docking, up and down the stairs. And, did I mention the cleaning? Scrubbing? And cooking? And, the *head*, don't even get me started.

"You want me to clean the what?" I asked Phillip.

"The head. With tiny tissues and Clorox wipes. Get to it," he replied, or at least that's how his reply was interpreted in my brain.

I know all of that now, but I did not know that then. While I am undeniably a hard worker and great cooker/cleaner/scrubber–even

when it comes to the head–at the time, I was admittedly new to this whole sailing business. Phillip knew he needed a good, trusty sailor, a "real salt," or two to help us make the crossing. While many were interested–apparently, for some, crossing the Gulf in a sailboat is a real bucket-list item–few could really take the time off from work to make the trip. It was going to be a five-day passage, at least, longer if the weather did not behave. And clever foreshadowing be damned here: she did not. When does she ever? After numerous phone calls and many a varied "thanks but I can't," we finally lined up a second mate–the soon-to-be-famous (after this rendition, anyway) Mitch. And, you may be thinking the more knowledgeable, sail-ready bloke steps up only as the *Second* Mate, not the First? You're damn right. Experienced or not, I was here first.

So, the 'we' was going to be three–Phillip, Mitch and me–who would be bringing the boat home. Our plan was to drive down the first day to stay in St. Petersburg, just an hour outside of Punta Gorda, the night before. We would then shake hands with Barb and Jack the following morning, get "the keys" to the boat, so to speak, stock and ready the boat, then sail out of Charlotte Harbor around noon. The first passage, from Charlotte Harbor to Clearwater, was about one hundred nautical miles, and we figured it would take us about twenty-four hours to make that run. *Yes, I say* we. While I had no sail experience, no idea how long it could, would or *should* take a sailboat to travel one hundred nautical miles–whatever those even were–Phillip and Mitch were cordial enough to include me in the "figuring" just for sport. I could at least tell by looking at the chart that the Charlotte Harbor-to-Clearwater run would likely be the easier of the two jaunts. We would be closer to shore and not traveling as far. Assuming nothing went wrong, it would be no problem. *Assuming.* After the first leg, we planned to tuck in for one night at the marina in Clearwater to rest up for the next leg–the true "Gulf Crossing"–where we would travel from Clearwater all the way across the Gulf and around Cape San Blas to Panama City, an expected two-day passage. This one gave even me a little pause. *What me, worry?* It was 218 nautical miles total from Clearwater to Panama City, the majority of which would be spent 100 to 150 miles offshore, hence the name: The Crossing. This was the huge jump, the big trip.

"If that don't get your fire started, your wood's wet," my dad would say. While that saying makes perfect sense to me, the same does not ring true for many of the other southern sayings I picked up in my youth. What it means, exactly, to be a "monkey's uncle," or "crookeder than a three-dollar bill," is beyond me. Your guess is as good as mine. But, I like the obvious ones. "Tighter than a frog's ass" means it's waterproof. "She ain't got a pot to piss in" means she's broke. Tack on "or a window to throw it out of" if'n she's really poor. And "madder than a hornet"–I know from personal experience as they are kin to alien wasps–means pissed off and ready to sting. Needless to say, this Gulf Crossing was definitely "getting my fire started." I was eager to get out there and prove myself. *I could do this!* I knew I could do this. I was, well, I was ignorant is what I was. Whether or not I could handle this sailing stuff was not based in any way on what I knew at the time, because I knew squat about what it actually felt like to be out there, 150 miles offshore, pitching and heeling over waves, forging ahead in the dark. I knew myself and my capabilities, but I didn't know the situation we were about to be thrown into. Like I said, I just needed to get out there.

Once we made it to Panama City, it was supposed to be gravy after that. One night in PC to rest up, then a quick twenty-four hour passage west along the coast of the Florida panhandle and we would be headed into the Pensacola Pass, bringing our boat safely home.

Nothing to it!

But, once we sat down with charts to actually plot out the passages, it finally started to dawn on me. *This was going to be quite the excursion.* Getting used to a new boat for the first time while simultaneously embarking on a five-day passage across the Gulf is kind of like putting a rookie team of astronauts together and sending them up to fix a satellite–particularly in my case, being the rookie sailor. There were so

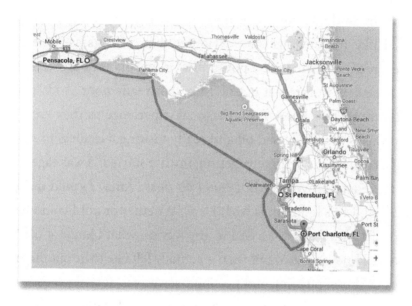

many systems on the boat I had yet to even figure out. All of those little toggles and switches and buttons. Some of them I knew their purpose but not how to operate them, others I had no idea why they were even there, much less what they did. There were so many components–the sails, rigging, lines, engine. Below deck there was the galley, stove, bilge and head. I disclosed my feelings previously about the head. Not to mention the safety gear–the life raft, flashlights, flares, emergency provisions, radios, electronics, batteries, on and on. We had to make sure all of that worked, could be fixed or could be done without and that we knew how to work, fix or do without it, all while sailing out there in the middle of the Gulf. Phillip kept calling it a "shakedown cruise" and I now know why. It was the shakedown of all shakedowns.

We spent weeks trying to think of everything we were going to need–from paper towels and soap to flashlights and flares, and *food*. My God! We were going to have to stock a whole kitchen from scratch. It was daunting. But the dates were booked. The trip was planned. Lists were checked, re-checked and double-checked and we had a big "passage pile" of necessary items growing in our living room. I was given repeated drillings on the EPIRB and man-overboard drills, and Phillip refreshed the weather report every hour it seemed for days, making sure we still had a good window of time where the weather and sea state were at least *predicted* to be fair enough to allow us to make the trip. This was it. And I was ready. I was going to use every bit of the grit and gumption I gained from my "shut up and eat it" Mom, my tobacco-spitting, story-telling dad and my creative and cunning brother. I may not have known how to sail the boat, but I was confident I could weather the storm.

And just as luck would have it. Mother effin Nature screwed us again! I can't help but think it every time: *That bitch!* As it always seems to happen, a pretty gnarly storm started brewing out in the Gulf just as we were getting ready to leave Pensacola to make the drive down to St. Petersburg. Phillip kept refreshing the weather data on his phone as we were packing up that morning, scrolling through it with a troubled frown. A storm was building and the sea state was expected to escalate to four- to six-foot waves and winds in the upper twenty-knot range over the course of the next few days. Yes, the very days we were planning to sail across the freaking Gulf from Clearwater to Panama City. *Of course! Stinking weather!* But, we had taken the time off from work, we had our Second Mate in tow and we were about to pile in the car to make the drive south. We were doing this. Maybe it would lie down some? Maybe it would pass through quickly or dissipate? Maybe. Whatever it did, we were still doing this.

Stupidly, I wasn't really worried about the weather in the sense that it might make for an uncomfortable, even dangerous sail. I can't explain it. Perhaps it was just ignorance or an unrealistic faith in the boat, but I had yet to develop any sort of fear for my personal safety during the trip. I just didn't think that boat could sink. I also didn't think it was possible for me to fall off and find myself irretrievably lost at sea. While I was well-versed on man-overboard drills thanks to the Captain, I didn't really think we were going to need to exercise one, not for me at least. I am a pretty sure-footed gal, having engaged in my fair share of athletic activities that require balance and agility–barrel-racing, gymnastics, cheerleading, rock-climbing, jello-wrestling. That last one probably actually requires the most agility. Everything is so slippery! But on the boat, there were so many things to grab onto, no matter what direction you were tipping, I couldn't fathom the possibility that I wouldn't be able to hang on. *I couldn't fathom.* The thought is laughable now. I was so ignorant.

But, even in my current, less-ignorant stage, I have to chuckle, because I still feel about the same. I find it a very rare moment indeed where I am fearful for my own safety on that boat. Even before my first passage, I found myself far more worried about the boat. Yes, the boat. Trust me. Get yourself a boat and you can easily worry yourself sick over it. Is that a leak coming from the engine? Why is that bilge pump going off again? Are those lines fraying? Is that a crack? There is plenty over which to worry. And, even then, before we ever set off, my worry for the boat was infinitely more pronounced than my worry for the crew, including myself. I was worried the bad weather, what Phillip kept calling a "rough sea state," would make for a passage that would be very rough on the boat. I knew how much this boat meant to him and how concerned he was about getting her back to Pensacola safely. I was sure four- to six-foot waves and twenty miles-per-hour winds might rip the sails, snap lines, the mast or, worse, break the keel off! *Was that possible?* Maybe. *That's* what I worried about. That damn boat. I still do.

What was my primary concern for myself? *Performance.* There were so many firsts at play on this trip–our first time sailing this boat on our own, our first time using the systems and learning the lines and rigging, our first time working together as a crew, our first time crossing the Gulf. Not to freaking mention, my first time to *ever* make a single passage on a sailboat, much less an offshore one like this. My primary goal was to learn quickly and perform well so I could become a dependable member of the team. Survival was way down on the list. Remember my thought process: *I'm sure-footed! I can't fall off!* Enjoyment was never a concern. Adrenaline pumped through me daily, jumping and snapping like a dog on a tight leash, eager to feast on the adventure. I was going to throw lines, raise sails and hold the helm with the best of them, eat salt for breakfast, lunch, *and* dinner. I imagined myself a real sailor. Salty waves crashed over me at the bow while I, knife in my teeth, tied some all-important knot in some all-important line to save the day. I also imagined myself looking like one of those classic pin-up babes in a tight little sailor outfit while I did all of that. *Who needs foul weather gear? It probably looks just like it sounds—foul.*

Finally it came time to actually depart. Because we needed a one-way ticket down—we were on a drive-down-sail-back mission—we needed some willing souls to shuttle us and all of our "passage pile" crap down to Punta Gorda. *Anyone? Bueller? Anyone?* Thankfully, Phillip's folks were up to the task—excited about it actually. They were thrilled Phillip had finally found his boat and they were planning to follow us along on the shore, stopping to meet up with us as we came into port at Clearwater and then Panama City, sort of like our very own "sailing groupies" if you will. We were thrilled to have them on board. It took some doing, but we finally got everything from the teetering "passage pile" packed up in the rental truck and hit the road in the early afternoon. It was a Wednesday.

While a truck might have been a good idea in theory, it proved anything but, in reality. We had to tarp everything down in the back in case it rained and then watch it flap and bounce around and generally cause trouble the whole way down. Also, our trusty second mate, Mitch, is about six-foot-four on a good day—definitely a tall drink of water. And, unfortunately, the rental was tiny on the inside, no bigger than a sardine can. Mitch had to eat his knees (even in the front seat) the entire nine-hour trip. I'd have felt sorry for him if he hadn't been so damn vocal about it. His rant started the minute we climbed in and was repeated every time we got out and back in along the way and every time he shuffled around in his seat trying to get comfortable,

hmmpph-ing and snorting the entire time. Cramped and tired from the trip, our bellies rumbling and Mitch grumbling, we decided to stop at a little cafe a few hours outside of St. Petersburg to stretch our legs and get some dinner.

By the time our drinks came, Phillip's Mom had made the whole wait staff, the hostess and the general manager aware of our sailing endeavors. She was one proud Mama. And she's the type who makes friends everywhere she goes. Within one minute of meeting someone, she's done told them where she grew up, how many kids she has, what they do for a living and, oh yeah, of course, "My son just bought a boat!"

"Now these three here," she said as she pointed to Phillip, Mitch and me, lined up like little kids at church on the other side of the booth seat, "they're going to sail Phillip's new sailboat–it's a Niagara 35–from Punta Gorda all the way back to Pensacola!" She would always make a big arc with her finger when she said "all the way back," and she would open her eyes so big you could see the whites on top when she said "Pensa-CO-la!" As I watched her wave her hands and widen her eyes, I couldn't help but picture Big Mom, back in that corner booth we used to always sit in at Doris's Restaurant up in Cullman, Alabama. She, too, always had her hands in the air, waving at somebody and practically shouting across the restaurant. "Just throw 'em in the bucket an' pass it along," Big Mom would holler across the dining area. Her own mouth full of 'em herself–chicken bones that is. Doris put out a big buffet every Sunday for lunch. She drew a massive after-church crowd, probably because a buffet is the best way to attract hungry Bible Belters. I mean, you've been sitting in a pew all morning thinking about that fried chicken. The thought of having to sit at a table, order it, wait for it and think about it some more is unbearable. No, we want to walk into a joint where you tell an apron-clad gal you want water, you don't care where she sits you, then you head straight to the buffet to fill a plastic plate. That's what Doris offered–no waiting for fried anything–and she made the best fried chicken in town. Savory fried flakes would break off when you picked up a piece and you would start salivating before you could even get it in your mouth.

Big Mom went to Doris's every Sunday after church and, much like Phillip's mom was doing now at the seafood cafe, made her presence known real quick. Every waitress in there knew her, as she did them. Big Mom would ask about their daddies and their mothers and whether she needed to take them anything this week if they were house-bound.

She would get and give updates on folks in the nursing home and talk about who she was planning to go see that afternoon. Then there was always the question about the sermon. "Did Preacher Mike give a goodun?" the Doris gals would ask her and Big Mom would always say, "The man is the mouth of God, I tell you." Then, after all those niceties were exchanged and it was time to make our heaping plates, Big Mom would set her buckets on the table—two grungy, gallon-size ice cream buckets. It seemed she'd been using these two, in particular, for years. The plastic on them was so old it was fogged and scratched up to a creamy white instead of the soft translucence it had once been. They smelled a little funny too. I know they got a washing every week. I saw Big Mom do it by hand, but they also got some serious use which caused a serious smell. I think she used the same two grimy buckets the whole time I was growing up.

Now, what were these buckets for? Table scraps, of course! It seems that might be a long lost art of the South, but all of the folks I knew up in Cullman, Alabama used to save their scraps. After a meal, they would rake whatever remained on the plate–unfinished bites, discarded bones, gristle, fat, pieces of bread, whatever–onto a designated "scrap plate" for the dogs or cats (or horses or pigs or goats or whatever other animals) they needed to feed. "Dog food ain't cheap," Big Mom would say to me as she pointed to the bucket, her greasy hands working a thigh, chicken and bits stuck under every nail, signaling me to slide my scraps in like the rest of the folk. While keeping a scrap plate around for every meal may have been a pretty common habit for most folks during that time, Big Mom, as it seemed she always did, took it one step further. Living through the Great Depression definitely has a way of making you not waste a thing. For Big Mom, a scrap plate wasn't enough. She needed a bucket–*two* buckets to be exact. About the time the after-church lunch crowd at Doris's was collectively starting to push their plates back and breath big sighs of fullness, Big Mom would hold up her extra bucket for one of the Doris gals to come pick up and start passing around–like the donation plate at church. And, most everyone knew what to do. Like I said, the folks who frequented Doris's often knew Big Mom and knew about her bucket routine, or they, as true Southerners, were simply used to the "scrap system." Everyone at the restaurant would scrape their scraps into Big Mom's bucket without even stopping their conversation–like it was a breadbasket being passed around the dinner table. "And then Johnny said to me," a guy would say as he took Big Mom's bucket from his son sitting on his left, "you can't use Uncle Timmy's mower no more," as he raked his chicken bones and leftover bits into it, "cause you didn't fill it up afterward the last time," as he passed the bucket to his wife sitting on his right, never missing a beat.

Big Mom's eyes would follow the bucket as it made its way from one table to the next, watching what folks was dumping in. Sometimes, on a very rare occasion, the bucket made its way to a table of newbies who hadn't yet been indoctrinated into the "scrap bucket system." They would take the bucket from whomever sat in the booth next to them, give them a quizzical, what's-this-for? look and peer into the bucket with mild confusion. Having watched the bucket at every pass, Big Mom would watch these folks extra carefully. If they didn't start raking immediately, she would raise a greasy, chickeny hand up in the air and holler across the restaurant, "Save 'em chicken bones for me!"

I always got a real kick out of watching the people look around at first to see where that raspy voice came from and then smile a bit when they saw Big Mom, her arm still in the air, flailing chicken bits all over our table as she'd holler again, "Save the bones. Put 'em in the bucket. Is for my dogs. Thanks y'all." I'd hide my smile behind a big chicken thigh and look over at dad who was just a-grinning too. Big Mom sure was funny. John would shrink down sometimes, all embarrassed like, but not dad and I. We were kind of proud.

I felt the same about Phillip's mom that night at the cafe. Kind of proud. She was so proud of Phillip for finally getting his boat, having planned this whole sailing trip from Punta Gorda "all the way," finger arch included, to Pensacola and having put together his very own crew to make it happen. I was proud of her being so proud of him. Apparently, her proudness rubbed off, because those nice folks at the cafe put us a special appetizer together—sweet and spicy conch bites—on the house, complete with a sailboat-themed setting to wish us well on our voyage.

As Big Mom would say, "Thanks y'all."

SEVEN

By the Moon

"You'll look like you've been in a motor vehicle accident."

She told me but I didn't believe her. It was Barbara, Jack's wife, the previous owner of the boat. I guess they would be considered 'previous' by that point. I don't know if actual ownership is exchanged when the papers are signed or when you stand face-to-face, shake hands and hand over the keys, but we were in the process of doing the latter when she told me. "I'm serious. Like you got T-boned by a Cadillac. You'll have bruises everywhere," Barb said. *Really?* I thought. Why was I going to get so bruised up? Everyone seemed to think I was going to fall all the time, bang into stuff, go overboard. I mean, *gees.* Who did these people think I was, Gomer Pile? I kind of smiled and forced a laugh. *Ha ha. Watch me. I'll hit nothing.* I heard her, but I didn't listen.

Barb was showing me around the boat below and helping me pack everything away. I was initially worried we weren't going to be able to fit all of the gear, clothing, equipment and food on the boat to actually take with us on the trip. But I was happy to be proven wrong. There were so many nooks and crannies, and inside those *more* nooks and crannies–plenty of space to fit everything we needed and more, and still have a clear walkway and living space. That boat was built for packing and cramming and, yet, still living. It was built for us! And, clearly it was built for Jack and Barb too. This was the first time she and I had been down in the cabin below together and I was shocked at how agile she was on that boat. I mean, she wasn't walking around with a cane or anything on land, but she looked to be in her late fifties or early sixties and of moderate health and agility when we met during the survey sea/trial. On the boat, however? She looked like a damn Cirque de Soleil contortionist, all grace and flexibility, passing like fluid from the saloon to the head to the v-berth. You could tell she really felt at home on that boat. Barb made it down the steps two at a time, squatted down on her haunches with ease to show me certain tucked-away cabinets and cubbies and hopped up onto the bed effortlessly to point out shelves and lockers where she liked to keep linens.

"Now, you may try to move everything around and put stuff in different places, but trust me, you'll do it, and then you'll try it one more way, and then you'll put it all back exactly the way I have it," she said. "Let me save you some time and just tell you it's all right where it needs to be." I had to laugh at that. *Well, she certainly would know.*

It really was kind of hard to see them there, watching us pack the boat up to take it away from them. Jack and Barb were super helpful, offering any tips and advice they felt could be useful for our first real trip, even standing in the makeshift assembly line Phillip, his parents, Mitch and I had made from the truck to the boat, passing along boxes and bags and containers. Jack had so much extra gear and parts for

the boat as well. Half of his garage was pretty much devoted to "boat stuff"–extra sails, rigging, lines, spare parts, back-ups for those spares, on and on. That man really took care of that boat. And Barb and Jack really took care of us. They made sure Phillip, Mitch and I were all packed and provisioned up before helping us aboard and giving the boat two nice pats. That was our cue. *Time to go!*

I think they were excited for us but a bit sad to see their beautiful boat go. We promised to take good care of her and they assured us if we did, she would certainly take good care of us. I hope, to this day, they feel they passed their beloved boat along to good hands. Phillip and I were certainly new to this cruising business, but we felt researched and ready. We set off around noon that day, heading out into Charlotte Harbor toward the Gulf.

The sailing was prime in the early afternoon. The sun was out. The wind was blowing eight to twelve knots and the waves were two to three feet all afternoon. We started to play around with the sails some and learn the systems. No matter how much you know about sailing, it always takes a bit to learn the rigging when you're on a boat that's new to you. For us, this consisted of a very complicated pull-and-wiggle approach where I would pull or wiggle a line from the cockpit and Mitch, up at the mast, would find the line I was expertly pulling and wiggling and determine what it controlled—the outhaul, or the boom vang or a reefing line, etc. We, of course, forgot most of that when it came time to reef (pull the sail down a bit) but it just takes a while. After we got the sails up and trimmed and on a nice tack, the crew took a collective breath and let the afternoon seep in. *See? This sailing stuff? Not so hard.* We put on some good music, made some good snacks and, did what all good sailors do–shed a few clothes.

Now, let me take a moment to tell you a little more about our Second Mate–the infamous Mitch. Where do I begin? First, I must say, he's an incredible friend to give up five days to sail across the open Gulf with us and help get the boat back. As fun as it is–remember what I told you about sailing. It is indeed hard work, and we were out of touch with the rest of the cellular world for days at a time. That's a big commitment and there is no way we could have done it without him. But, as I mentioned, Mitch is all of six feet, four inches. While that may seem pretty normal for a guy–on land–it's a bit much on a thirty-five-foot sailboat. Mitch lumbered and bumbled around that boat like an elephant going through a carwash. Each step of his foot on the deck sounded like Neal Armstrong landing on the moon. *Kaboom.* I honestly felt sorry for him while I watched him bumble up and down the companionway stairs and through the hatch. He must have felt like he was crawling around on Playskool equipment.

After a while, Mitch decided to give it up altogether. Instead, each time I got up to go down the stairs, and I mean the *minute* I merely lifted my ass off of the cockpit seat, he would start in with: "While you're down there." Sometimes I just had to screw with him. "Down where, Mitch? I was going up on the deck to check the sails," I would say as I walked up topside, knowing full well I'd had every intention

of going down below, but whatever it was for was now going to wait another fifteen minutes until the next time Mitch beckoned. I have to admit–it was fun–and Phillip and I had a good time christening him with the nickname–Mitch, While-You're-Down-There, Roberts. But, to be honest, I'm sure it was a lot of work for him to lug that big body up and down those tiny stairs, and he did hold the helm for several shifts that day, so the teasing was always followed with, "Sure buddy. What do you need?" Mitch was a talker and a screamer but he had a heart of gold. He taught me a great deal about sailing and he was a true asset on the trip.

One thing he didn't have, though, was a poker face. If Mitch didn't like something, didn't want to do something, or didn't agree with something, you didn't have to guess at it. If he didn't tell you outright, his face would. He'd squish it all up in mock (or genuine) disgust and usually let out a big "hmmpph" to go along with it. What caused this face the most? The drinking water. While we do it differently now–they call it a shakedown cruise for a reason–on that trip we drank water from the tanks on the boat. Think of it as our "tap water." While tap water at home I actually prefer–I think all of the fluoride and other chemicals really give it that something extra–on the boat, the tap water tastes like piss, like water that's turned. The best way I can describe it is like a cooler full of ice and beer and bottles–people reaching in it all day with their dirty hands, cans and bottles bobbing around. Then imagine it three days later, having sat in the hot sun on the back porch. The ice has all melted and the water's been sitting tepid, with little bits of hot dog and potato chip crumbs floating around in it. Pour that up in a re-used water bottle–the plastic all white and fogged up like Big Mom's scrap buckets–and that's about what the "tap water" on the boat tasted like. But, we had to stay hydrated, so we suffered through it. Phillip and I did so in silence. Mitch did so with a squished-up face and a "hmmpph." Every time he took a sip, he would smack his lips unsatisfactorily and hold the bottle up in the air eying the little particles floating around in it suspiciously. I kept watching him smack and swish, smack and swallow, "hmmpph" and smack again and it took me back to Big Mom's dining room–that Christmas that she made the rum cake. We were all sitting at the table: my dad, Aunt De, her son, Chuck, John next to me and Big Mom at the head until she had scooched away from the table in a huff and went to the kitchen to do some smacking and swishing. Then we heard her voice roar through the house like a freight train–"John drank my RUM!"

I'd say John was somewhere around the ripe age of eighteen or nineteen–the time in your life when you're spending your days taking some kind of dumb associates degree classes at the local community college and waiting tables at night–and he was living with Big Mom at the time. It seems we all did a "stint" with Big Mom during our lives at one point or another. And, I call it a stint because it was very similar to doing time. While Big Mom was very generous to open her doors to her many kin in various states of broke, newly divorced, kicked out, stranded or otherwise transitioning, she had a pretty severe set of rules when you stayed at her house. Most of them involved kitchenware–what glass you were supposed to use, when to use a paper plate instead of an actual plate and when to throw your paper plate away. I assure you, it was not after every use. The first three times you were to rake the crumbs off and put it in the half-used paper plate pile. Not until you reached the fourth or an unquestionable amount of times, whichever came later, were you to actually throw the paper plate away. Big Mom also had a specific method for loading the dishwasher–back to front, always–and her unique blend of "plasticware"–grungy, stained, decades-old Country Crock and Cool Whip tubs she used as tupperware–always went on the top rack. There were also rules about keeping your room clean, getting your dirty clothes "down the shoot" in time for the wash, curfew, bedtime, which was different than "T.V. off time" and plenty more. I did a few months in the "Big Penitentiary" right out of high school and it was enough to last me a lifetime. John did a year or two around the same time in his life, but he was never one to get marks for good behavior.

During his first stint, John managed to find his way into Big Mom's liquor cabinet while she was at church one Wednesday night and had himself a merry time with the rum. Now, Big Mom wasn't really a rum drinker–these liquors were more for baking than anything–brandies, sherries, etc. The rum, in particular, was set aside for her record-breaking, world-famous rum cake! Okay, maybe the cake wasn't *world* famous, but probably famous in those three counties up there that always seemed to get together for a tri-county fair, especially since they were dry counties. Imagine if the secret ingredient in your Bundt cake was cocaine. Folks would go wild! The rum made Big Mom's cake super moist. It was so good, you almost felt a drunken high after finishing a slice. Even my young little rumless palette could appreciate it. Unfortunately, though, after John had himself a smashing good time that night with Big Mom's baking rum, he then had the smashing good idea to fill the bottle back up with water. *She'll never know*, he probably thought. It's clear, looks the same, has a faint rum smell from the bottle. *No one will be the wiser*, John thought.

Big Mom decided to make rum cake for Christmas that year and she spent hours in the kitchen meticulously crafting her tri-county award-winning culinary treat. She made the frosting herself, used her special round cake pan, the whole nine yards. It smelled fantastic and looked fantastic. But it didn't quite *taste* fantastic. I mean, it tasted alright. It just didn't have that usual Big Mom flare. As we all sat around the dining room table, nibbling on our pieces, ensuring her the cake was still really good, Big Mom kept mulling each bite around in her mouth and swallowing slowly, knowing it wasn't really good, it wasn't even regular old good, in fact it wasn't right at all. So, she went to the source. The rum. We all leaned over at the table so we could see her in the kitchen tasting the rum. She would take a swig, swish it around her mouth a bit, swallow with a frown and hold the bottle up to the light to inspect the clear liquid–much like Mitch was doing now with the tepid water on the boat. It didn't take long for Big Mom to realize it wasn't rum at all, and with John being the only one living with her at the time (and probably the only one stupid enough to fill the bottle back with water), it didn't take her long to figure out who the culprit was. She puffed her lungs full of air and let out a roar from the kitchen.

"JOHN DRANK MY RUM!"

It was funny but Big Mom delivered it with such force, shaking the house with her rage, it wasn't allowed to be funny. She stormed into the dining room where we all swallowed a collective bite of bland water cake and she gave John a good, solid lashing–right there during Christmas dinner. It was a holiday that went down in the books. Several years later, when Big Mom was getting up in age, I decided to surprise her one year with a lighthearted holiday roast based on the "Twelve Days of Christmas" song. We did "Twelve sayings of Big Mom" instead: "On the first day of Christmas, Big Mom said to me …" I wrote down twelve of our most memorable Big Mom sayings on little pieces of paper, we threw them in a hat, drew and sat in a coordinated one-through-twelve circle, with Big Mom at the pinnacle, to sing the song. As each of our "Christmas days" came up, we would contribute our drawn "Big Mom saying." While there were many of them–the calling birds, French hens, and turtle doves were replaced with "Always use your glass," "Save your paper plate," and "Load from back to front"–my favorite will always be the one we swapped out for the five golden rings. After the Big Mom colloquial replacements for seven swans a-swimming and six geese a-laying, we all shouted at the top of our lungs: "JOHN DRANK MY RUM!" This was immediately followed by:

"Always use your glass," by my cousin Chuck.

"Save your paper plate," by my dad.

"Load from back to front," by my aunt De.

And, the partridge? Well, I did write the darn thing and cut up all of those little squares. That was tough work! So, I did some home-cooking with the hat-drawing and made sure I got number one. On the first day of Christmas, you know what Big Mom said to us?

"Save the-emm chicken bones for meee!"

I chuckled at that memory as I watched Mitch continue to smack his lips and force down every putrid sip of water. I had to let him struggle through a bottle or two plain before I pulled out the Dasani water additive–quickly dubbed the "squirt stuff"–which finally saved him. After that, it was: "While you're down there, will you get me a bottle of water?" And then he would always add, "Oh, and do the yellow stuff this time, the … mango whatever." *Sure Mitch. No problem.* He was quite the character on the boat, but he certainly was a trooper to help make this passage with us. With all systems running smoothly we were making good headway toward Clearwater that afternoon. Everyone was settled in comfortably as we watched the sun set over the bow of the boat and congratulated ourselves on an excellent day of sailing.

I got industrious that evening and labored away on some sweet potato chili in the galley. Remember all of those books we had ordered? All of those hours spent on the couch reading and studying? Well, some of them were galley cookbooks with plenty of easy, throw-together recipes for the boat. The one I chose to make that night? Sweet potato chili. What it would forever be remembered as? Broccoli Crappola. We'll get there. At the moment it was a miracle I hadn't blown up the galley and, in the process, had somehow made us a warm, satisfying meal to help fuel us through the long night ahead. The sun had just set and Clearwater was still another fifteen hours away, but the crew was full and content for the moment and eager to make way. I curled up in the cockpit, a warm bowl of chili steaming my face and I watched the stars as they started to pierce through the black veil above.

"How do you see at night?" I remembered asking Phillip one evening in the weeks before we left. I had been reading and devouring exorbitant amounts of information on dock lines, sail trim and anchoring and it was the first time it actually dawned on me that we would be sailing through the night–the dark of night.

"Do we have, like, headlights on the boat?" Yes, I seriously asked that. I figured it might be like a car cruising down the interstate, something that could shine out and at least give us visibility of one hundred feet or so. Surely. Otherwise, how would you do it? Just barrel forward into the black abyss, staring only at the screen of some bat-like signaling device that would satisfy you there was nothing standing in your path? What if a passing ship didn't have their lights on or didn't show up on your magic bat radar? Or what if there was some other inanimate object that wouldn't register–an unknown land mass, an oil rig, an ... iceberg? Okay, an iceberg was unlikely in the middle of the Gulf of Mexico but I was genuinely concerned.

The thought that you could just see, with your naked eye–the water, the horizon, the path ahead–never crossed my mind. Do recall this "headlights" question came from the same girl who thought they would be delivering our boat to us. Looking back on it now, I realize Phillip had every right to tilt his head to one side and pat my head slowly like a lame dog, but he just chuckled–a lighthearted, patient chuckle before he responded. And, while the answer Phillip gave me seemed impossible at the time, as I sat there, cupping my bowl of chili and looking out on the horizon as the night set in, I realized it was true. It was happening right before my eyes. So many features–the choppy texture of the water, the entire length of the boat, the mast, the sails, even a dolphin in the distance–emerged. And I could see them all! Just as Phillip said I would: "By the moon." It's amazing how clear your night vision becomes when you're that far from shore. Without all the glare and glow of city lights, the moon and stars, and their reflection on the water, illuminate everything. I could see the entire boat–all the way up to the bow–and for miles out across the water. And, I could hear her, slicing through the waves, making way in the darkness, powered by nothing more than the wind. Everything was amplified. My senses heightened. Night sailing was an invigorating experience of sight and sound. The crisp smattering of stars overhead, the gentle rocking of the boat and the cool night air whispering across my face took me back to another cool night, on the farm in Alabama.

"But, how can we? Its ... It's so dark we can't see." My dad was hoisting my little body up onto his horse in what seemed to me to be the pitch black of night. He had just turned off the camping lantern we used to mend the fence and the immediate shift from brightness to dark made me feel blind. I couldn't see the saddle. I just straddled out of instinct, fell onto it and gripped my hands around the worn, slick leather of the horn. A neighbor had called my dad that afternoon and told him he'd seen a few head of dad's cattle on the other side of the fence up by Briscoe Hill. So we had rode up together, through the thickets and steep terrain to bring the cows back in and fix the fence. Unfortunately, the job had taken longer than expected and we worked through sunset. Now, here it was, the sun was down and our only way home was back through the difficult terrain on a horse in the dark.

"But," I started one more time but dad stopped me.

"It'll set in, Babes," he said. "And don't you worry. The horse has her footing." I heard but I didn't understand. Just as I had when Phillip told me "by the moon," I wanted to protest—the lawyer in me, I suppose. *But how? It's too dark. I can't see.* But, I had just said those things and he had already answered. I had no other questions and I trusted him. I gripped the horn, still trying to blink my vision back, as dad settled in behind me on the saddle. He gave the horse a soft cluck and we started back down the hillside. It was strange, at first, to feel the horse move forward into the dark without being able to see where she was going. A light grip on the reins told me we were in control, but it was the horse who was carefully picking her way over the dark terrain. We simply had to sense which way she was going to lean or move and

move and sway our own bodies along with her for balance, just like we were doing now on the boat.

After a while, though, small pockets of sky began to peek in through the trees and I could see a massive sea of stars above us. As I brought my eyes down, branches and leaves started to appear. I could see rocks on the left, a fallen tree on the right and, finally, the mossy path before us came into view. Just as dad said it would, it was setting in–by the light of the moon. I rode the rest of the way in peaceful silence, making out soft shapes in the dark, my body gently moving and leaning in rhythm, because he was right about that too. The horse definitely had her footing. As I sat there in the cockpit remembering that night–the same cool breeze dancing on my face, the water, boat, sails and horizon having now sufficiently set in–I was surprised to feel myself, even on the first night, starting to build the same kind of trust with the boat. We were in control. We were guiding her by the light of the moon, but it was the boat who had her footing. It was she who was leaning and rolling, carrying us over the dark waves.

EIGHT

By the Stars

"Around 340, 345," Phillip's voice broke through the soft tread of the horse on my memory lane. "Try to hold it there." Mitch and Phillip were doing a shift change, and Phillip was handing the wheel over. I thought about it a bit, trying to conjure some good sailing sense from all of my studies. If 270 degrees was due west and 360 degrees due north, then Phillip's "340, 345" mandate was, roughly, a north-northwest heading–right about the direction we should be headed if we were trying to make it along the coast from Charlotte Harbor up to Clearwater. And, I was actually proud of myself for it. *Hey, I know what direction we're traveling. The real* cardinal *direction.* This coming from the gal who could never accept a cardinal direction on the streets was a pretty impressive feat. I hated when people told me: "Yeah, head west about a mile then go south till you see McDonald's." *West? South? Please.* I would have scoffed at such a ridiculous offering for help–on land. That's because east, west and north made such little sense to me on land. When my days were filled with interstates, intersections, highways, and fast food chains, it mattered very little to me where the sun rose and where the sun set. But, when you're out on the boat, in a huge body of water, where there are no interstates, intersections, or land McMarkers to go by, it's all so simple and matters a great deal. If the sun rises on your starboard side, easing up slowly, sliver by pink sliver, between your bow and the big winch that holds the powerful reins of the Genny, then you know it will set on your port side behind the stern. Because one is the east and one is the west. You know this because you are keenly in tune with the direction in which you are heading and the direction from which you've come—a sense that, to me, is utterly lost in the blinding glow of cities and fast food signs.

I was glad to see Phillip stand and stretch. He had been holding the helm most of the day with Mitch giving him only intermittent one or two-hour breaks here and there. But it was now nearing 10:00 p.m. and Phillip was getting justifiably tired. I had held the wheel briefly at times throughout the day—when the two of them needed to go up together on deck to do something with the sails—but it was clear Phillip was a little reluctant to give up the wheel, even to Mitch, and especially to me. I just hadn't done it before. Steered a sailboat. Sure, there was a wheel that you turned to the right and turned to the left, but it was very little like driving a car. First, the response time for the boat is a little delayed. You turn the wheel to the left and a second or two later, the boat will *start* to respond. Waiting for the boat to do what you just *told* it to do can be a bit unnerving if if you're on a collision course or headed toward peril. Also, when the boat is under sail, you have to stay within a limited range or you'll backwind the sails, accidentally jibe, get yourself in all kinds of trouble pretty much. You're also battling waves and the current and looking out for a possible shift in the wind. You're keeping an eye out on the horizon for other ships, crab pots, buoys, floating debris, that random iceberg–anything you could possibly smash into and, once again, get yourself in all kinds of trouble pretty much. It just wasn't as simple as keeping the sails full and following the course. There were so many things that you had to look out for, account for, and be ready for. I was undeniably new to it, so Phillip was justifiably cautious in handing over the "reins" to me during this initial shakedown passage. But, I did offer, every time he and Mitch changed out, although it probably appeared much more like the "courtesy reach" for the wallet when the check comes, because–truth be told–I was kind of scared to death to hold that wheel. Well, not scared of holding the wheel as much as I was afraid of what was sure to happen the minute *I* grabbed the wheel–a rogue wave, a big gust of wind, a whale or a pop-up oil rig right in front of us. Something was bound to jump out at us and cause me to do the exact wrong thing in a panic and roll the whole boat completely over. I was sure of it. But, I offered despite my fear. And I did want to learn to do it despite my fear.

The boys were taking two-hour shifts during the night–one of them serving as the helmsman, steering the boat, while either I or the other boy stayed up and kept watch with the helmsman for two hours–then trading out. Until I earned my stripes as a night helmsman the only help I could offer was to stay up with them most of the night, talking to them when they got sleepy and helping to keep an eye on the horizon. I did feel a little guilty about it because I knew it was far more work to hold the wheel and I could tell the boys were exhausted.

Hell, I was exhausted. Yet they were still getting up, every 1-2 hours, all through the night, to take their shift, hold the wheel and keep us on course to Clearwater. If I really wanted to sail this boat with Phillip all over the world, I figured now was as good a time as any to start contributing as a real member of the crew. I watched Mitch for a while as he held the course, noticing the range he stayed in–anywhere from 338 to 348–never outside of that. I watched him make tiny little adjustments on the wheel–just a smidge to the right, a smidge to the left, very small increments–to hold an average heading as Phillip had instructed in the 340-345 range to keep us heading north northwest.

Phillip was still awake with us in the cockpit. I felt like he had only gone below deck three times–maybe–the entire day. 93.46% of the time, he was glued to the wheel. And, even when Mitch was on shift, he was glued to the cockpit. Phillip sat in the cockpit, he ate in the cockpit, he slept in the cockpit. As we all did most of the time. I could definitely see now why Phillip was adamant about the comfort of the cockpit. It *was* like our living room. It was definitely where we lived. And, now it was where he slept. About an hour into Mitch's shift I watched Phillip as he finally started to nod off and I was so grateful, both for the fact that I knew he needed sleep–we still had a long way to go that night and an even longer way to go the next time–and because I felt I now had my chance.

"Psst, hey Mitch," I whispered, giving him the finger on the lips signal–the keep-it-down cue.

"Yeah, what do ya need?" he asked, thankfully, heeding my 'shush' instruction and responding in kind, in a light whisper, glancing at

Phillip.

"Let me give you a little break there," I said, watching his face to see what he thought of my offer. *Was I really trying to help or was I just curious? Did he really want to hand the wheel over to me? Did he think I could do it?* I was thinking he was thinking all of these things, but turns out–he wasn't. Mitch loved a break, no matter how it came.

"Great, thanks," he said as he practically hopped out from behind the wheel. Then I was a little scared. Half of me thought he would do what Phillip always did and politely decline. Half of me didn't think he was actually going to stand up, hand over the reins, and pat me on the back. Half of me thought he would wave me off, but nope–not Mitch. He was happy to accept. "Here you go," he said, as he eased out from behind the wheel, careful not to wake Phillip, his hand fingering the wheel until I had a good grasp on it.

Phillip rustled around just a bit as I wriggled in behind Mitch and gripped the wheel. I sat down, looked out, and gave Mitch a little finger-curled come-hither signal. He leaned in. "Just stay around 345 or so, right?" I asked. "Nothing else to it?"

"Nothing else to it," he said as he kicked back on the other side of the cockpit.

Nothing else to it, I told myself. *Nothing. Else. To it.* I felt a little empowered sitting behind the wheel of that boat. Here I was, first-time sailor, my crew kicked back safely resting, and I was in control. *I was* steering us across the great, big Gulf. Mitch was, of course, on watch with me, staying awake, looking out, making sure I didn't add anything "else to it" and get us all goobered up, but he was lounged back with his hands woven together behind his head, definitely relaxing. And, there I was—really doing it. Sailing that boat in the middle of the night, in the middle of the Gulf. I have to say, it felt pretty damn cool.

Pretty soon, though, it stopped feeling so damn cool. Holding a heading in the dark is like trying to play Atari for the seventh hour straight. Your eyes are already exhausted and our GPS is mounted by the companionway, about four feet in front of you. To hold your heading you have to keep your eyes locked on those numbers, turning the wheel a little to the right when the number starts to drop, and a little to the left when the number starts to increase. That was it. That's what you did. For hours, in the dark, staring at that screen. I guess Mitch finally took pity after he watched me for about a half hour, hunched over the wheel, my eyes locked on the GPS, trying to blink away the irritation and monotony of it.

"That's not the only way to do it, ya know," he told me. *Do what?* I thought. *I'm steering the boat. Isn't this how you steer the boat?* I loosened my hands a bit and realized how hard I had been gripping, leaned forward, staring intently at the bright numbers on the screen. I wriggled my fingers and stretched them out a bit. My silence a cue to just let him talk. If I was doing this the hard way, I certainly wanted him to tell me the easy way—the sooner the better.

"You see that star, there?" Mitch said. "Put it on the tip of the sail and hold it there." I watched his hand as he pointed out a star sitting just above the horizon, a nice bright one. Mitch kept his finger on it, his arm and hand holding a steady point, while the rest of his body bobbed and moved slightly with the motion of the boat. He was holding the star. And, every time the boat came down gently, the corner of the genoa sail would land just about dead on that star. I watched it land a time or two in a row and watched Mitch as his eyes shifted from the star, to the GPS, back to the star, then back to the GPS, making sure we were holding the heading by holding the star. I could feel myself falling into a nice rhythm, making adjustments as needed to keep the tip of the sail on the star and soon I found myself looking less and less at the GPS and actually holding a steadier heading than I had before with the blink-and-squint method. Soon, I was just looking out on the stars–the bright one included, our "heading" star–but the rest of them as well, all at the same time. I was moving the wheel out of instinct, watching the night sky and the horizon. My night vision returned and I could see, once again, the glistening choppy water, the sails, the mast, the moon. It was beautiful. Now *this* I could do for hours–sailing by the stars. "Sight sailing," said Mitch. *That too,* I thought. Either way. "Much better, huh?" he asked. I nodded quietly in agreement, enjoying the serenity of it, the at-oneness. *Yes, Mitch. Much better.*

I stayed on another hour or more and there was a brief moment where it was just me. Me and the boat and the water and the wind. Both boys shut their eyes for two minutes–I counted–and I was in complete control. It was a good kind of scary. Probably because it only lasted two minutes. But, I relished in it, gripping the wheel tight with clammy hands, watching that star bounce and land every time near the tip of the sail, smiling without realizing it. *I was doing it.* Sailing. Across the Gulf. At night. I was *really* doing it. For two whole minutes.

"Well, look at you," Phillip said when he finally rustled, rolled over and realized it was me at the helm.

"Look at me," I said with a proud smile. *Look at me.*

Phillip stood and stretched and took over. But for those last two minutes, Mitch had stayed awake next to me the entire time and I had done it. Held a shift. A night shift at that. Little did I know at the time that those were pretty much perfect conditions–a gentle breeze around eight knots, blowing directly across our starboard beam, nice two- to three-foot following seas, clear skies–truly ideal sailing conditions. It was the last we would see of them on this trip, but even in those conditions, I was still tired from the shift. There's not much to it other than holding the wheel and looking out but it is still tiring. I guess because you're doing it at like three in the morning. I could see how enduring several shifts like that a night could really wear you out, but I could also see how it could be done–two people, cruising along in a boat, even overnight. I now knew you could see at night. I knew you could cook, eat, and sleep comfortably on a boat. You could travel for hundreds of miles without fuel, a motor, or any power source other than some canvas into the wind. I knew that I could do it. As I laid back and finally closed my eyes to take my turn for rest, I was starting to sense not only that I could, but that I *liked* doing it. So far.

That was until I woke the next morning and made my way to the head. I won't go into detail but suffice it to say one of our crew members needed a little more instruction on head care. You put water in the bowl, you add your own "stuff" to it, then you pump the water and stuff into the holding tank. If not all the stuff goes down, you add more water and pump again–like flushing a second time when you've got an obstinate floater. It's not rocket science. Even I understood it. Someone else, however, did not. When he saw me hunkered over the bowl, working away with a handful of Clorox wipes and a decidedly-not-dainty face, he offered a short apology.

"Well, you shouldn't have fed me all of that broccoli crappola last night," he said.

Broccoli? BROCK-olee?! I screamed inside between scrubs but said nothing. When I came out a few minutes later, having worked up a solid sweat scrubbing that damn bowl, I wiped a swath of sticky hair from my forehead intentionally using the back of the hand that displayed the crumpled-up wad of browned Clorox wipes and looked straight at him.

"It was sweet potatoes, Mitch," I said. "Sweet potatoes," as I threw the used wipes away. He smiled lightly and shrugged his shoulders up a little. It was all I could do not to smile back. I scrunched my mouth tight, holding it back with all of my might, and he knew it. We never talked about it again but I put a big can of Clorox wipes near the head and never found it in that condition again either.

We were all in pretty good spirits when the sun started creeping up on the horizon that morning. It felt like an honor to be sitting there, watching it, as if the sun was putting on a special showing just for us—only three in the theatre. We brewed a rich batch of coffee and sat in the cockpit, each warming our faces and hands with the mugs and watching the sun burn the sky a brilliant pink.

The wind began to pick up that morning as well. We watched, at first in excitement, as the sails filled and started moving us along.

The excitement soon turned to worry when full became taut and taut caused the boat to groan and heel steadily over. The wind continued to build so we decided to reef the sails for good measure. I insisted Mitch let me help so I could learn how to do it. The more time I spent doing things that actually controlled the boat, and doing them right *enough* so far, the more my confidence grew, the more I began to envision just Phillip and I doing it (no offense to Mitch), and the more I wanted that. I needed to learn.

"Did you really just slap me?" I asked Mitch.

"Well," he responded. *Well.* That was all. We were both trying to wrap the furling line for the Genny around the winch to pull her in a bit as the winds increased and I guess my hands, in doing the job, seemed to keep getting in the way of Mitch's hands, in doing the job, and he saw fit to slap one.

"Okay, I did, Girlie. But I didn't want you to get your fingers caught in there. And you were wrapping it wrong anyway," Mitch said. "Look, I'll show you." And show me he did. Mitch taught me how you have to wrap the line clockwise on the winch or it won't work, how to keep my fingers out of the way so they wouldn't get–you know–mangled up in a bloody mess when the Genny sheet pulled taut. Perhaps the slap was helpful after all. He also taught me how to cinch the line in the cleat to hold it, and how you have to un-cinch it before you start to pull it again. You may have thought that one would have been obvious but *well.* He also taught me how to let the outhaul out and pull it back in, how to reef the sails, how to adjust the sails, how to tie the mainsail down. I was learning, and Mitch was teaching, the only way he knew how–first with a slap, then with a light scold, then with all of the reasoning behind it.

"Girlie," I said. "I'll show you girlie," as I grabbed the line, wrapped two quick loops–clockwise this time–around the winch and gave a mighty pull which was followed by a mighty "ping." Just as my sailing confidence was building it was shattered. *What had I done? I* thought. *What did I just break?* We all looked at each other sternly, wondering but not asking: *What was that?* And it was clear none of us knew. I secured the Genny line and began looking around the cockpit for some kind of clue when I found it lying on the cockpit floor–a bolt head. And I say a bolt "head" because the bolt had sheared right through, just below the head. The bolt stem, if they call it that, was nowhere in sight. I picked up the bolt head and held it up for the boys to see, hoping they could give me some kind of answer–an easy, "Oh, that's the bolt to the such-and-such. That's nothing to worry about," perhaps. But they didn't. They both just stared at it with no answer, their heads starting to shake from side to side. And so I just stared too, with no redemption. I was the one who had been pulling when the ominous ping occurred. I couldn't help but think I had pulled too hard and broke some almighty important bolt on the boat. *What had I done?*

NINE

Surely Loctite Can Fix This

My brother, John, and I used to play this game called Psycho. Probably because we were—a little bit—but it was a pretty intense game. It had to be played at night or you had to at least hang a thick blanket over the window to block out all of the light if you wanted to play during the day. We sometimes nailed one up there for just that purpose. It had to be pitch dark in the room so that you could hide from the "Psycho," whose job it was to find and nab you in the pitch dark before you made it to the door and hollered "Safe!" The game involved a lot of scrambling over furniture in the dark, some wrestling, tickling, punching and sometimes crying. It was an awesome game. On this particular day, John and I decided to play it in the daytime before Mom got home from work, which required the blanket procedure. We scooched a chair from the kitchen to John's room to stand on to nail up the blanket. While you may think the nailing was going to be where we got nailed in this story, it was actually the chair—that stupid, flimsy, particle board-backed chair.

Our dinette set growing up, if you can call it that, was a mishmash of four chairs–one with a high back, no arms and a swoopy wood design on the back. Two were office chairs–basic metal tubing with seats that looked like they were upholstered with your grandma's couch cushions–and the other was an old captain's chair that looked, ironically, like it should have been mounted behind the helm of a boat. It was a very nice set indeed. John and I always used the high back chair for the blanket-nailing because, with the right balance and the right

counterweight on the seat, you could stand on the actual *back* of the chair to reach the top of the window–usually anyway. That's not how it went down on this day, though. I was sitting in the seat as John stepped up on the back of the chair–a hammer and a wadded-up corner of blanket in one hand and a nail in the other–John started to ease up to the window and the chair let out a weak cracking sound. I leaned up a little, afraid we were breaking it. We hadn't yet, but we were about to, because when I did, John's weight on the back sent the chair tipping instantly backward, quicker than I could stop it. The chair fell back onto the carpet, I fell onto it and then John fell onto me. Why I always find myself at the bottom of a human heap when accidents like this occur is beyond me. When John crashed onto me, I crashed through the back of the stupid swoopy wood crap on the back of the chair, and I swear my brother said "Shit!"

Now I wouldn't say Mom was any harder on us than she needed to be. Okay, maybe just a little, but breaking something definitely deserved punishment, no matter how it happened. You shouldn't break stuff, right? But, if you break stuff while using it in a way you're not supposed to while hanging things you're not supposed to hang while using a nail and hammer to do it, which you're not supposed to use, you're pretty much asking for a whipping. Mom mustn't find out quickly became objective number one for John and me. We propped the chair back up and started picking the wooden pieces out of the shag carpet. It was just cheap, pressed plywood with a shiny lacquer finish but it was in

about twenty pieces. John and I started trying to fit the stupid pressed pieces back into place to re-create the swoops on the back of the chair and it seemed it was going to be possible, but we needed something to make them stick. *Glue, glue,* we were both saying to ourselves as we stormed the house, looking for some type of bonding agent. That was a pretty common childhood thing, right? Lots of kids have construction paper, scissors, glue and glitter. Arts and crafts after school! You would think. But, for whatever reason, we didn't. John and I couldn't find any Elmer's anywhere, no Krazy Glue, no Lee Press-On Nail glue, nothing. We dumped the junk drawer in the kitchen, the one where you keep tape, pens, ribbon, Sharpies, scissors–all of that typical household crap that needs to go in one drawer but nada–no glue-like substance anywhere. So, we raided my step-dad's little shed-of-a-shop behind the house, checking in every one of the drawers of his monstrous Snap-On tool box looking for something that would promise to stick two things together and hold them for life! Then John found it.

"Loctite," he said as he read aloud. "Construction adhesive for indoor and outdoor use. Applies white, dries clear." John held the big tube up and turned it around before his face a time or two inspecting it. It had this huge gun, trigger-like contraption on it. I had no idea how you made the glue stuff come out but John pulled the "trigger" a few times and it wasn't long before a white blob smushed out. We both kind of looked at it, not knowing what to do. I touched it, of course, to see if it was sticky and it was. The "touch test" had to be enough. Mom would be home in about thirty minutes, and as it stood now, we had a shattered chair in John's room and a shaky future if Mom saw it. Loctite it was. John and I worked quickly to piece and glue back together the retarded swoop design on the back of the chair. I have to say, in the end, we did a pretty damn fine job. Aside from the little white veins and rivers running between the freshly-glued pieces, it was almost unnoticeable and, as promised, the product dried clear. Like many of the stupid things John and I did in our youth, the many things we broke and glued back together, Mom never found out about this one and that chair held for decades. It's still there, in our little linoleum-floored kitchen, creaking every time someone sits down in it. That Loctite stuff is no joke.

And I swear to you, that's the first thing that came to my mind when I picked up that sheared bolt head from the cockpit floor. *Loctite.* The word was so clear, I almost said it out loud. *Surely Loctite could fix this,* I thought. Surely I could somehow glue this almighty, important bolt head back onto its little bolt body and fix this! I almost said it to the boys, half joking, but I don't think they were in a joking mood–half or whole. There wasn't anything that was going to fix this. Wherever this bolt had come from we needed to get another bolt in there quick.

I began looking around the Genny cleat and the winch where I had been working when we heard the ominous "ping" but saw no clues. Every bolt in that area seemed to be fully intact. We were confused but without the luxury to worry about it at the moment. As we began to make our way into the Pass to Clearwater, the wind had picked up to about twenty knots with seas building. Our primary concern was to find the marina and get docked and secure as soon as possible. We would worry about the bolt be-heading then. We had already pulled the Genny completely in and reefed the mainsail. A tiny little sliver of canvas was all we had up but it was still too much. It was taut and surprisingly powerful for a sliver. The boat was trying to put her shoulder into it and hold her course into the channel but the winds kept pushing her off track. Imagine trying to walk a straight line perpendicular to the wind while holding a big piece of plywood over your head. It was just too much surface area. We needed to drop the main entirely and motor to safely maneuver the narrow pass into Clearwater. I hopped up on deck to help Mitch drop the sail. This was both the first time we were dropping it on our new boat and the first time I was helping to drop a mainsail, ever. And this time there was no scolding and no slapping! Phillip eased out the main halyard from the cockpit while Mitch and I wrestled it down.

"Help fold it up as best you can when it drops," Mitch was telling me. "The lazy jacks will catch it some, but try not to let it topple off the boom if you can." Surprisingly this made sense to me. All of it. The lazy jacks, the boom. I was starting to speak "sail." I had even brought up the sail ties knowing we would use them to tie around the mainsail at three points to hold her in place. Once Mitch and I had stacked the sail up on the boom, I pulled them out of my shirt front, bit down on two of them–the green frayed ends flapping out of my mouth–and started tying the third around the big wadded up stack of sail near the mast. Mitch stood there, watching me with mild curiosity.

"What," I said through clenched teeth, bearing down on salty, green sail ties. "You want to tie one?" I finished the first tie, pulled the others out of my mouth and held one out to him.

"Nope," he said, waving his hands in a lighthearted decline. "You seem to be doing just fine." *Girlie*, I thought to myself as he turned and made his way back toward the cockpit. I licked the salty fabric flavor the ties had left on my lips, a smile forming on my face without my even knowing it. *I read the books. I know what I'm doing.* Truth was I half did and half didn't. I had some sail wits about me—from studying all those months, sure—but I didn't know how serious the conditions could get out there. The wind was whipping across the boat as I was tying the sail ties and I had to keep my arms around the boom to hang on. The sea state wasn't too bad yet, maybe three- to four-foot waves, but it was enough that you couldn't stand without holding onto something. "*Three points of contact,*" I remembered Phillip telling me. "Anytime you go up on deck, you always want three points of contact." At the time I thought it was kind of funny. I imagined myself standing on my hands near the mast, touching the boom with a toe and saying, "Like this, Phillip? Three points?" But, it wasn't funny now. As I held on to the boom, the wind pushing my chest onto it and felt the boat kick and jump over the waves below, I could see how three points could become four and then how four could become six. I imagined myself this time crawling on my hands and knees up to the bow in torrents of rain, gripping anything attached to the deck as the boat heaved and bucked over monstrous waves. As I now understood how possible it was, the image of it appeared vivid in my mind. If we got out there in the wrong conditions, I knew that's exactly how it would look. And Phillip was right. There was nothing funny about it.

Even after we got the sails down, the force of the wind on the boat was still noticeable. "Bare poles" Phillip had called it. When all you have are sticks–basically your mast, stays and shrouds–up in the air and your boat still has enough surface area for the wind to push it. We were heeled a little to port with just bare poles. It was clear we needed to take cover soon. The Gulf was brewing up something awful that day. *This is what he was talking about,* I was thinking. When we were making the drive down to Punta Gorda and Phillip kept refreshing the weather report on his phone every five minutes, talking about the sea state, the winds, the "conditions" offshore. Now I was getting it. But these weren't "conditions." That sounded like such a playful little term now. No, these were hell-breathing Sirens of the sea, trying to tip our sticks-only boat over into the churning abyss. I thought back to the day Hook-Mouth had taken us out in that teensy little bay with full sails up and let the wind heel us over. That seemed like a gentle summer breeze. If we'd had the sails up on our boat when *this* offshore bitch came blowing through, our mast would have laid right down on the water. My hands gripped the sail ties in as much of an effort to tie the sail down as to hold on. The wind pressed my chest harder and harder onto the boom and my legs rode the boat over rocking waves like a galloping horse. Here, now, in this moment, I was finally getting it–why these so-called "conditions" were so respected among sailors, so revered.

As soon as we had cell signal, Phillip told me to call the marina and get directions. I got on the phone with a man named Lou. His voice was thick and garbled–like he either weighed three hundred pounds or was talking through a mouth full of marbles. He was the dockmaster, and I swear they must all be cut from the same cloth (at least down there in South Florida) because I talked to many during the course of this trip and they all had similar one-syllable, car mechanic names (Dick, Bob, Lou, Joe) and spoke with the same garbled dialect. They gave directions just like my dad would—not with precise streets to turn on and miles to travel before you'll see your exit. No, they use obscure, only locally-known markers like "take a left after Briscoe Hill and head toward Johnson's barn." *Thanks dad, big help*, I would say to myself as I cursed him, winding my way lost through back country roads. These dockmasters were exactly the same.

"Come in through the pass until you go under the big bridge," Lou said. "Then hang a left and you'll see our marina there with the fuel sign." Yep, that's as clear as it got. And, I even asked him—like a dumb blonde asking for directions—"the *big* bridge?"

"Yeah, honey," Lou replied with a huff and a chuckle. "The big one. There's only one, but it's *big*." I knew I wasn't going to get anything else out of him, so I simply relayed the message exactly as it was told to me and hoped Phillip could make sense of it. Thankfully there was only one bridge and it was undeniably huge and noticeable, although I don't think it required the "honey" prefix. We went under it, preparing to "hang a left" shortly thereafter. I will say while I know now how stressful docking can be—particularly when you're coming into a new pass, to a new marina with a new crew—at the time, I had no clue. I just knew Phillip was tense and stern—all business—and focused entirely on the GPS and the depth readings. I knew our primary focus was not to hit bottom—dig our keel, in other words, into the rocks or dirt or whatever grimy Gulf bedrock was underneath us. I knew our boat was approximately five feet, two inches deep, although with all of the gear and people aboard—one of whom was six-foot-four Mitch—I knew I was supposed to mentally tack another six-or-so inches onto that for good measure. I also knew "deep" wasn't the right word for it. It was "draft." And that when you got careless and navigated your boat into waters too shallow for your draft—thereby hitting said bottom—this was called "running aground." You might think I knew a lot.

I did not. I knew squat. I didn't know what it felt like to actually run aground, how bad of a thing it really was, how you got out of it—assuming you could—or how to prevent it other than not going in water too shallow for your boat. But what if the water *got* shallow all of a sudden? What if the charts and GPS were wrong? What if there was something down there—a sunken pirate ship or whale carcass or something—that wasn't picking up on your fancy sonar equipment? It's not like we could *see* down there, like we had one of those spiffy back-up cameras for the car mounted down there. I just shouted out depth readings periodically to Phillip, not knowing what else to do and thinking perhaps that could be helpful. That way he would at least know, at that very moment, we had enough depth. The next moment and the moment after that, I could make no promises. Pirate ships and whale carcasses could be abundant. Mitch was up at the bow looking out for the "left" we were supposed to "hang" at some point and he saw a marina just off the portside of the bow. It was far more "dead ahead" than left but how far is too far? We didn't know.

"That's it. Up there. That *has* to be it," Mitch shouted from the bow. "Head that way!" Phillip eyed him cautiously, looked back at the GPS, back up at Mitch and stood fast for a minute. His mind racing, his eyes darting around. I knew he was worried, anxious, but I didn't know how to help and I kind of hated that I didn't. Thinking I was all big and bad tying some darn sail ties up there when here Phillip was, dealing with the actual problems: navigation, depth, shoals, tides, boat traffic–you know–the real stuff.

"No, uh-uh," he said finally. First kind of to himself, then out loud, "No. I'm not comfortable with this. And if I'm not comfortable with it, we're not doing it." I just sat there kind of dumb-like. Okay, not kind of but *actually* dumb-like. *Well, if we're not doing* it, *what* are *we going to do?* I wanted to ask but didn't.

"Here, Annie, take the wheel. I'm going to check the charts," Phillip said as he started down below.

Oh shit, I thought. *You want* me *to drive? In twenty-knot winds? In a tight little pass? Are you out of your effin mind?* That's what I thought but not what I did. I took the wheel and checked the GPS. Thankfully I was learning enough by now to know the first thing you did when you took the wheel was to get your bearings and figure out where you were going or, better yet, where you *needed* to go to keep the boat safe. We looked pretty clear for the time being–no intimidating objects or boats near us with a pretty wide, safe range on the GPS–for the time being at least. Phillip plopped the paper charts up onto the cockpit seat with a thud and plopped right down next to them to figure out where this damn marina was. Then I saw it come up on the screen, looming ahead of us like an ominous blob. "There's a shoal ahead," I said to

Phillip and pointed, so he could see it too.

Phillip looked at the screen and started shaking his head. "You see? That's exactly what I'm talking about," Phillip said. "Turn around and go in a big circle."

"I, I ..." I started to ask him which way I should turn, and then I wanted to ask him if there was anything behind us (when I was perfectly capable of turning and looking myself) and then I thought about whining a little: "Why are you making me drive? Why do I have to turn?" And then, thankfully, I did none of those things. Phillip was stressed enough as it was, trying to pick our way safely through this pass for the first time, trying to deal with a new crew, new boat, and new territory that he was "not comfortable with." I certainly didn't need to solicit his input right now on which way I should turn. I looked around, saw we had a pretty big clearing around us—fortunately there wasn't a ton of boat traffic zipping through the pass right then—chose port and started to turn. As soon as I did, Mitch came stomping back to the cockpit, hollering, "Why are you turrrning?"

When he got back there and realized I was driving and Phillip was poring feverishly over the charts, though, he asked no more.

"Look," Phillip said, pointing it out to all of us on the map. "There's a huge shoal up there, right in front of our path to *that* marina," with a point toward the marina Mitch had spotted on our port bow. "We'll run aground."

Mitch looked solemnly at the charts. There was no way he could have seen the shoal ahead standing on the bow and he was trying to help by pointing out a marina he saw ahead that was arguably *somewhat* to the left. Mitch didn't apologize but he didn't need to. His silent acceptance and continued efforts were enough. Mitch started looking around for another marina as I turned the boat again before we made it back to the bridge (yes, the *big* one), but neither of us could see anything else on the horizon that looked like a marina. Not knowing previously what a marina on the horizon would look like, I at least knew now from what Mitch had spotted on the port bow, that it looked like a big patch of sticks coming out of the water. They were sailboat masts–all bunched up close enough together on the horizon–so you could tell it was a marina. I now saw it. But I didn't see another.

"Here." Phillip was pointing it out on the map. "There's one around this bend to the left. That's where we need to go," Phillip said, etching our path with his finger. We couldn't yet see it because it was tucked away behind the bend. Remember that "left" we were supposed to "hang." But as Phillip took the wheel and started easing us around, the masts came into view. I felt a collective wave of relief wash through the cockpit as we all eyed the big red-and-white fuel sign at the dock–the one the dock master had told us about. This was our marina and we had a clear path to it. There was even a big overall-clad, corn-fed lad standing there by the sign waving us in. *That had to be Lou! Whew.* The worst part was over I thought. I *thought!* I should have just stopped all that damn thinking right there, because the worst was yet to come.

Lou walked the dock along with us, showing us where our slip was and waving us in. The winds were really blowing by then–about twenty knots coming across our port beam–as we made our way toward our slip. "The wind's going to be on our stern as we're coming in," Phillip said. *Our stern.* I knew that was the back of the boat but I sat trying to hide my look of confusion as to why Phillip had said that as if it was a bad thing. *Wouldn't it be harder if the wind was pushing us out of the slip, not into it?* But, I didn't dare say a word. Mitch didn't seem to share my confusion, so I didn't vocalize it. I was sure it was mine and mine alone. Mitch was heaving dock lines and fenders up to the bow as I tried to recall any one of those dozens of docking diagrams I had studied. I was trying to remember the names of the lines. *There's a stern line, a bow line.* Those made sense. *What's that one in the middle called?* I couldn't remember. The words wouldn't come. *Shit!*

"Annie," Phillip broke through my internal docking jumble. "You're going to take this one." I felt relieved when he handed me the stern line. At least I knew what that one was called. I even knew it was on the port side. *Okay, yeah. I got it. The port stern line.* "Now, you see the poles at the end of the slips," Phillip was pointing at a slip a few ahead of ours to show me as an example.

"Uh-huh," I said cautiously. I was afraid of where this was going. I was "not comfortable" with the pole.

"We need you to catch that pole with this line." He said it as if it was no big deal—as if he had asked me to "toss this ball into that bucket." As if it could easily be done, or that if I wasn't able to do it, it was nothing to worry about. Just pick up the ball and try again. I started to believe him that maybe it was going to be easy. *Just catch the pole. No big deal.* Then he ruined all of that when he said, "You've *got* to get that pole."

The way he said "got to" freaked me out—the emphasis he put on it.

I was all of a sudden baffled by the thought of *catching* the pole. *What exactly did he mean by that anyway? Hug it? Get my line around it? Snare it in a net? How does one* catch *a pole exactly?* Now I was nervous but, nervous or not, it was happening now. Phillip started to turn and there was the pole. *You've got to get that pole,* I told myself. I made a big, baggy loop with the dock line, thinking I could just toss it over. I realize now I thought nothing about what I would do after, assuming I *did* get the pole. Was I going to just hold both ends of the line, all of my weight against the force of the boat? I had no plan for pulling the proper slack and cleating the line after I got the pole, again assuming I got the pole. But, fortunately, I didn't have to worry about any of that, because I didn't get that fucking pole. I kept flailing and tossing that line and it kept dancing and jumping and only intermittently hitting the pole, bumping the pole, even high-fiving the pole but never–as Phillip had told me I *had* to do–"catching" the damn pole. I tried, as many times as I could until the pole was out of my reach and I had failed miserably. We had no stern line, and we had twenty-five-knot winds coming on our stern, practically shoving us into the slip. Only then did I realize why it would have been exceedingly better to have the winds pushing us out of the slip instead of barreling us into it. I knew Phillip had the engine in reverse and was gunning it but our little engine-that-could was no match for the inertia of our fifteen-thousand-pound boat with freight train winds on her back. We were charging ahead toward the dock with no way to stop the boat.

By the grace of whatever marina Gods exist out there, Dockmaster Lou–who was a rather large farm boy himself–had an even larger brother, whom we learned later went by the name of "Red," and he was standing there with Lou when our boat came barreling in. They each gripped the pulpit on the boat and pushed and strained with all of their might. It looked like we had two sumo wrestlers pushing our boat off of the dock, only they were in overalls not those weird thong/belt things that sumo wrestlers wear.

"Bring back the springer," Phillip hollered to Mitch. *The springer,* I thought. That's the name of that other stinking line. *Why couldn't I have been in charge of the springer? I would have been brilliant with the springer!* My stupid pole that I was supposed to get was now ten feet behind the boat and Lou and Red's faces were turning a bright crimson at the bow. Mitch came jogging back, grabbed the springer, wrapped it around a pole near the cockpit and pulled hard. The boat pulled hard to port and groaned into the dock. As Lou and Red kept pushing, Mitch was able to pull more line around and pull our bow back finally. With the boat secure, Phillip took my stern line and caught my stupid pole in three or four throws.

I was crushed.

I knew I had really let them all down. If Lou and Red hadn't been there, our boat would have smashed right into the dock. There would have been nothing else to stop her. I was supposed to catch that damn pole. *Why couldn't I catch that pole?* I had thrown plenty of ropes in my days–even roped some with my dad. I was a country cowgirl, and you're telling me I can't even lasso one stinking pole when it really matters? I was pouting and apologizing over and over to Phillip, until he finally cut me off.

"It's alright. It's hard to do," he said. "But shut up about it already. We're here. It's fine." I hung my head and pouted some more. I knew he was right. Phillip usually is. He is willing, and always encourages me, to try anything. But he doesn't piss and moan when things don't work out or when he doesn't get it right on the first try. "The trying is what it's about," he tells me. But I just couldn't shake the guilt and embarrassment. "Girlie," I mumbled to myself as we were picking things up around the boat and packing shower bags.

"Get over here, Girlie," Phillip said, as he pulled me in close. "Not many *girls* would have made that trip as well as you." He pushed some dirty salty curls away from my face and kissed my forehead. "I think you're getting a little saltier," he said with a smile. I didn't know whether he was talking about the salty layer of muck that had caked my face from the wind, waves and overnight passage or perhaps a new nautical stripe I had earned from having survived the wind, waves and overnight passage. Either way, I felt better. I finally eased up, cut myself a bit of slack and stopped pouting–as much.

"Boy, you came hauling in here son!" we heard Phillip's dad shout from the dock. Our sail groupies, Phillip's parents, had made it to Clearwater the day before and had been waiting for us to make our way in from the Gulf. Phillip had planned to text them after we docked and got settled but that didn't turn out to be necessary as they had been wandering the docks most of the day and had witnessed our embarrassing entry for themselves. Apparently–as Phillip's parents often do–they had already told everyone at the dock about us. "Phillip, my son, he's an attorney, he's coming in on a Niagara 35 sailboat!" his

mom had told anyone who was willing to listen. Everyone already knew who we were, where we'd come from and that it was our *first* time docking our *first* boat! I'm surprised more people didn't pinch our cheeks and tell us how cute we were. Phillip's dad had even gotten a dock report from Lou and Red before making his way over to our slip. *Sheesh*. But, I guess that's what groupies like to do. *Brag*. They lined us up in front of the boat and starting snapping shots like the paparazzi, documenting the event—our first overnight passage.

Our groupies had also rented a hotel there near the marina and we unapologetically took full advantage of the facilities. After a full twenty-four hours on the boat with little sleep and spit baths only, a hot shower and a nap were our first order of business. Well, maybe the pool was first. As soon as we walked up to it, we couldn't be stopped.

Layers started coming off and we jumped right in. There's no better feeling, after being on a salty, restless, overnight passage, than diving into a cool pool of crisp blue water. We paddled around for a bit but showers and food were still high up on our list. It was a quick dip and then a three-stage shower procession. Feeling clean and scrubbed and new, we headed back to the boat for an easy snack dinner, wine, then rest Glorious rest! The crew was beat. But we had done it—made our first passage. And the boat was somehow still floating and—thanks to Lou and Red—now docked, secure, and relatively unscathed. The crew was also alive, secure, and relatively scathed. And we were in Clearwater! It was one step closer to home with our big, new beautiful boat.

We did have some hard decisions to make though. The twenty-five-knot winds we had experienced in the protected waters of the pass were only a glimpse of what it was like out in the Gulf. The storm had

rolled in and brought cooler temperatures and some rain. It was still blowing a steady twenty- to twenty-five knots in the Gulf with five- to seven-foot seas, predicted to last two to three days. As Phillip and I laid in the v-berth of the boat, I tried to really imagine what a seven-foot wave would look like coming up to the boat. *Is that seven feet from the water, or seven feet from the deck of the boat?* I wondered. Stupid questions, I know, but that is honestly what I was thinking. The image of me crawling along the deck in sheets of wind-driven rain, dragging some rope or sail by my gritted teeth flashed in my mind again—this time with a *seven*-foot wave climbing above me on the starboard side. Surely that's what we would look like out there. Now that I had actually been there—topside on the boat in howling winds, struggling to do something as simple as tie the sail down in conditions half as

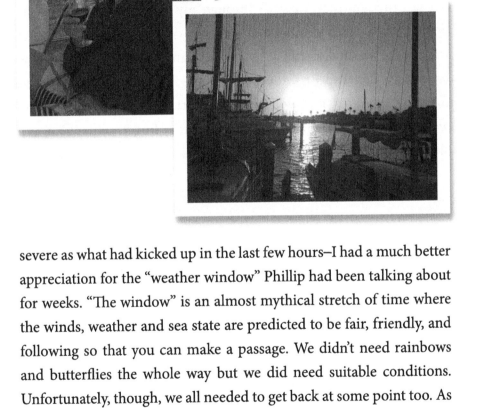

severe as what had kicked up in the last few hours—I had a much better appreciation for the "weather window" Phillip had been talking about for weeks. "The window" is an almost mythical stretch of time where the winds, weather and sea state are predicted to be fair, friendly, and following so that you can make a passage. We didn't need rainbows and butterflies the whole way but we did need suitable conditions. Unfortunately, though, we all needed to get back at some point too. As it seems is always the case, time was of the essence. All of us had jobs to get back to and we still had another four to five days to get home, even after we left Clearwater. We couldn't risk getting out in the Gulf in the current conditions, but we also couldn't wait in Clearwater forever. We knew we would likely be staying one more day and night at the marina, at least, in hopes that the sea state would calm down during that time. But, if it didn't. *Well* ...

As I finally began to shut my eyes and feel a deep sleep set in, the last thought that "pinged" through my mind that night was the bolt. We had planned to look around the cockpit for a headless bolt the minute we got docked but in the chaos and calamity of the docking itself–with Lou and Red, the botched pole-catching and all–we had forgotten all about it. I wondered for a brief moment what the bolt went to. But it didn't take long before I, too, forgot all about it and slept–for the first time in twenty-four hours–a deep and glorious sleep.

TEN

Mattresses and Parachutes? That's Crazy Talk

I heard a creak then a floorboard pop then a camera snap. You know that sound. That unmistakable "kuh-chuck" and you *know* some moment in time has just been memorialized forever. What was our moment? It was our very first night on the boat together. Our first time to sleep in the v-berth. And don't get any ideas. We just slept. That is all–with the door open and Mitch snoring five feet away on the starboard settee. It was also my first time ever to sleep on a boat. I would love to say that I woke gently to the soft sounds of birds chirping on the bow, slowly blinking myself out of a deep slumber, yawning, stretching and smacking like a cute bunny in the woods. But, no, I woke to a kuh-chuck and a, "Wow, it sure is cozy in here!"

It was Phillip's dad. I kid you not. He was there with us, standing in the v-berth, taking pictures when we woke up. Scratch that, when he woke us up. Kuh-chuck. Kuh-chuck. He had the best of intentions, trying to document our first trip together on the boat. But he had woke up well before the crack of dawn that morning and brought all of those intentions right down to the dock, right down the companionway of our boat, and he was now *having them* right there with us in our bedroom for all purposes, at six in the morning.

"How does it sleep?" he asked, still snapping. Kuh-chuck. Kuh-chuck. Phillip was just ignoring him, so I felt I could, too, my eyes shut tight in mock sleep. But it wasn't working. "Can you stretch out? Can you shut the door?" That was Phillip's cue. He smacked his mouth into working order, sat up a little in the bed and finally responded.

"Yeah, dad, you can. Let me show you. Take that door there," he said, pointing to the door to the v-berth. Phillip's dad looked up at the door nodding. "Now, unlatch it on the back."

"Oh, neat. Here?" his dad asked.

"Yep, right there. Now pull it toward you."

"Cool, like this?"

"Mmm-hmm," Phillip said patiently. "Just like that. Now step back behind it."

"Okay," as he eased out of the v-berth, the door shutting in front of him.

"Now, keep pulling it until it shuts," Phillip said. His dad—now muffled from the other side of the door—finally caught on. "Oh, I see what you're doing … "

"Yep. We'll see you in a bit dad."

His dad muffled out a sad "Oh alriiight," and clicked the door shut. I listened as he made his way back up the companionway stairs and into the cockpit, where I imagined he would sit until we woke up, taking another twenty pictures. I didn't hear Mitch move a muscle the entire time. I doubt the impromptu photo shoot stirred him a bit. He was a slumbering beast. When I made my way out of the v-berth later, he looked like that guy on *Gulliver's Travels*—a giant all roped down to the ground. His feet and one arm stuck off the side of the settee and one wadded-up little sheet was tangled all around him. That man was just far too large for any boat. It took several shakes and a hot cup of coffee to rustle him up.

We made some mugs and started walking the dock, chatting with several other boaters here and there. And while I did not know then, I certainly know now—the cruising community really is quite small. You'll meet folks in a remote anchorage down in the Keys who have met the couple that keeps their boat next to yours at the marina. "You know Bob?" they will ask. "The guy that wears the captain's hat all the time? And, his wife Sherry, with the … " (I'll let you get creative with that one). And, you'll smile and nod, "Yes, yes. We met them last summer out near Dog Island. They keep their boat nears ours now at the marina." And while you get used to it, kind of, you can't help but smile and shake your head each time and say to yourself: "Small world." The "small world" encounter we encountered that morning, however, was an almost spooky coincidence. The three of us—Phillip, myself, and Gulliver—were walking along the dock when Phillip ran into a guy he knew from Pensacola. Yes, *there* in Clearwater, he bumps into an old neighbor of his from back home. While that may not be too uncommon, there's more! Phillip gets to chatting with him and learns that he's there helping a friend, who just bought a boat down in south Florida, sail it back to Pensacola. *Crazy.* That's exactly what we were doing. Small world, huh? But wait, there's more!

"So, where did he buy the boat?" Phillip asked.

"Punta Gorda," his friend answered. "We sailed out of Charlotte Harbor and up the coast yesterday and we're going to make the jump across the Gulf to Apalachicola as soon as the weather lays down."

What? So are we! Small friggin' world. It was also a very beneficial coincidence to boot. While sailing across the Gulf in a sailboat isn't the most dangerous thing in the world, it isn't exactly the safest either. As is the case with most semi-dangerous sports–scuba diving, rock-climbing, hiking–it's always safer to do it with a buddy. That way you've got someone else there with you, watching your back, making sure you make it safely down to the wreck, up to the top of the boulder or, in our case, across the Gulf of Mexico. Having a buddy for a passage like that really is smart. Now, we'd met ours–the *Bottom Line* guys–a crew of three on a thirty-two-foot Seaward Unlimited named *Bottom Line*.

We chatted them up a bit, discussed the sad state of the weather, and talked about our plans for crossing the Gulf. We all agreed to stay in Clearwater that day to wait out the worst of the storm with hopes that we would be able to head out the following morning. Whether we left the next morning or the next, though, we knew there was a chance we were still going to face some serious weather out in the Gulf–likely fifteen- to twenty-knot winds and four- to six-foot seas. The image of that seven-foot wave popped back up in my mind towering over the side of the boat, about to come crashing down on me and knock out all six of my points of contact. A *six*-foot wave is only one foot shorter than a seven-footer. I was sure it still packed about the same punch.

"We better ready the boat," Phillip said after we bid the *Bottom Line* guys adieu and were walking back along the dock to our boat.

Ready the boat? I thought, not knowing exactly what that meant. I tried to conjure some remote chapters from some of the textbooks I had read in preparation for this trip to see if any of them could shed some light on this mysterious "readying," but nothing came of it. I honestly flashed back to the days when my brother, John, and I used to drag one of the twin mattresses from our bunk beds out to the backyard so we could land on them while trying to parachute off of the roof. However, our version of "parachuting" was holding the four corners of one of our twin sheets in our grubby little hands and jumping. We fully expected the sheet to pop out full above our head when we leapt into the air, carry us gently down–back and forth, on a gentle summer breeze–and drop us all dainty- and feathery-like on the mattress below. That's how it happened in the cartoons anyway. Needless to say, that's not what happened when John and I did it. Instead the sheet would flog uselessly behind us as we kicked and flailed and sunk through the

air like a rock. Hence the need for the mattress. I always wondered if Mom ever noticed the grass and dirt that was caked in the crevices and corners of our mattress. If she did, she never said anything. But the mattress was key. Before I would jump, I would always holler mightily down to John–"Is the mattress ready?"–to make sure everything was in place for me to make the leap. As if a foot of padding is going to help much when you've got a good twelve feet of dead drop before you get to it, but it seemed to. Miraculously, we never broke anything. But we certainly never parachuted either. That was the first version of "ready" that popped into my mind as we walked the dock. We had a boat–a good, solid, dependable one allegedly. What sort of mattress-scooching would we need to do to better "ready" her for passage?

Thankfully Phillip's memory of the mysterious "readying" textbook chapters was far better than mine. He started talking about strapping down gear, getting out the storm sail, and securing the dinghy on the back of the boat. *Yeah, those things.* I had totally thought about those things. *Mattresses and parachutes? That's crazy talk.* Phillip got Jack, the former owner of our boat, on the phone to ask him about a few of these things. The dinghy was held up by davits on the back of the boat with the outboard engine attached to its transom. This worried Phillip because it was a lot of weight suspended on the back of the boat. The dinghy weighed about one hundred twenty or so pounds, and the outboard was another thirty or so, which meant approximately one hundred fifty pounds swinging around behind the boat. It was also off-balance with the outboard on the port side. Jack told us, though, that he always kept the outboard on the dinghy on the davits–even on passage. When he sold the boat to us, he did not have the plate mounted to the stern rail of the boat that held the outboard. Meaning, even if we wanted to take the outboard off the dinghy for the passage, there was no real good place to put it. Could we store it below? Send it home with Phillip's parents? We worked through these possibilities, but Jack assured us he always traveled with the outboard on the dinghy on the davits, that he had strapped the dinghy securely, and that we shouldn't have a problem with it. After twenty years owning, maintaining, and cruising that boat, we couldn't help but think: *Jack was the expert, right?* So, readying the dinghy. *Check.* Next item on the agenda.

Jack also told us how to rig up the storm sail, which I did recall from my studies–probably because it has one of those great obvious

names that doesn't require too much thought. I'd love to have a chat with whoever came up with the port and starboard references because *that* took some time and some ridiculous rhymes to get down pat. The best one I could come up with was the word right has more letters than the word left. Same's true with starboard and port. You see? It's not funny, cute, or easy to remember. I plan to have a talk someday with the port-starboard guy. The "storm sail," however, is an aptly-named smaller sail used when sailing in high winds that accompany a what? A storm, lad! Hence the name! We decided to spend the day rigging up the inner forestay, which the storm sails hanks onto, and try raising and lowering the storm sail to make sure it was all in working order before we left the dock and headed back out into the Gulf.

Although it was a smart thing to do, it was a futile endeavor because just as we were pulling the halyard to raise the storm sail the inner forestay snapped and the sail fell in a loose heap on the deck. The line Jack had rigged as the inner forestay hadn't been used in years. Unfortunately it was so old and dry-rotted that it broke right in two. Not only was the break a serious morale blow, the loss of time stung too. We had spent several hours trying to rig the storm sail, so it was disheartening to see it all just fall in a depressing pile and know the time was lost. But it couldn't be fixed. We had no way to run a new forestay up through the mast ourselves—particularly not there at the marina in one day. So, Phillip decided to forego the storm sail and just secure everything else as best we could for rough seas. Everything on deck was bungeed and strapped down and everything below was put away, strapped or otherwise confined so we wouldn't have any equipment, clothing, or supplies rolling around the cabin floor in rough seas. While I understood what we were doing and why, I couldn't quite fathom the actual need for *all* of it. Seriously, the boat might tip over so much that this heavy bag of flares and flashlights and junk will slide right off the settee? *Seriously?* I was doing it, everything I was told, and everything I remembered from my studies, tying and strapping and securing things, but just like when John and I used to jump off the roof, a huge part of me really did believe that sheet was going to pop open and float me down like a piece of tissue paper. Part of me didn't think we needed the mattress at all. But, I would holler down and check it all the same. "Is the mattress in place?" I don't think I would have actually jumped without it there. I don't think. What are all of those sayings? Better safe than sorry. Safety first. Don't test fate. *Okay, the mattress it is.*

So I kept tying, strapping, and securing and after a tiring day of readying the boat for passage, the three of us were beat. We kicked back in the cabin while the Captain starting putting together an incredible batch of shrimp feta pasta for dinner. It was the first time I really got to "hang out" and have dinner on the boat–like you would do if you were anchored out somewhere. My first night on the boat I had swayed and rocked while cooking up a pot of "broccoli crappola" under way, the remnants of which I also had to clean up the next morning in the head. The next night, we were so tired from the overnight passage, Phillip, Mitch and I ate snacks–tuna dip and crackers I do believe, real gourmet–in the cockpit and crashed out immediately after without even brushing our teeth–real hygienic. Now here we were, tied up

safely at the dock, the three of us tucked away in the warm cabin below, sharing a bottle of wine, and getting ready to cook dinner. I watched and listened as Phillip lit the stovetop, pumped water into a pot for the pasta, got a wooden spoon out of the drawer and started cooking up a nice, hot meal in the kitchen—or, the galley. On the boat, it's the galley, but it felt just like a kitchen.

I pictured the little linoleum-floored kitchen back in the house I grew up in in New Mexico, the corner of it peeling by the stove. I could see my brother seated in one of the plaid office chairs as I sat in the highback swoopy chair (before we broke it) next to him while my stepdad, whom we called Pa, cooks us up some fried pork chops in the skillet we always hand-washed. Our dog Jiggs has worn a butt imprint into the rug in front of the stove next to Pa's feet. She always sits right next to him when he cooks because he hands little fried niblets down to her when mom's not looking, although we all know mom knows he does it. I could see my mom opening a can of some "Great Value" veggie to dump in a pot to go with the chops, using that crank can opener with the pointy tip on the end she always used to punch a triangle hole in a can of tomato juice to add to her beer. Mom would always set the veggie can down on the table in front of me before dumping it because she knew I liked to drink the "veggie juice" out of it first. I still do. Pea juice is my favorite. Corn's a close second.

I could hear the sound of the silverware drawer as it opened, the sound of the grimy little plastic silverware tray as it banged to the end, and the clang of the can opener as mom put it back in the drawer. You know all of those sounds that start to become so familiar when you've lived somewhere for so long? You can sit in the next room over and know exactly what someone is doing in the kitchen simply by the sounds. I could imagine getting used to all of the sounds Phillip was making here, in the cabin of the boat–the sound of the stove lighting, his wooden spoon banging on the pot, the little fridge on the boat slamming shut. It wasn't just a galley. It was a kitchen too. *It* could be a home too. Phillip, Mitch, and I huddled up in the cabin around piping hot bowls of pasta, big glasses of red wine in hand, laughing, talking, telling stories, and I started to think *this* is what it could be like–living on a boat, traveling the world, in our own little mobile marine home. *We have to do this!* But first, we had to get her home.

ELEVEN

Who Has the Gorton Pants?

In college, I drove a car that started with a screwdriver. It was a fire-engine red four-door Ford Escort and, to crank it, you had to use a screwdriver–a flathead to be precise. I was waiting tables at Cracker Barrel at the time and I came out one night after my shift to find my car wouldn't start. The key would stick in and turn but it wouldn't do anything. I called my dad who came in his old green Dodge Ram and "towed" me–with a big rope and a stern lecture on braking-while-being-towed–to a nearby auto shop. The boys at the shop spent a half hour taking apart my whole steering column only to tell me it was going to cost four-hundred-and-something to fix it. *Four hundred?* I barely had forty in the bank at the time. Even counting the sticky wad of bills shoved in my apron from my last shift, my sum total was still shy of a hundred. I knew dad wasn't in any better position either. So, there I was. Stuck at the shop, my car seemingly undriveable, facing a bill I couldn't pay. I must have been a sight, traipsing around in my stained brown apron–four gold embroidered stars and my name at the top–angry, irritated, scared, and practically cursing the head mechanic guy because of it–very unbecoming of the Barrel.

The head guy didn't seem to give a shit, though, because he just let me rant to empty air while he stepped away to "take a call." I hadn't heard a phone ring. When he went back in his office, I stomped outside for some air and when I did a big, greased-up black mechanic stuck his head around from behind the garage doors, looked around a few times all suspicious-like, and said, "Folluhme." So, folluhhim I did. He took me back to my car–the column all exposed and mangled. A little white round plastic piece with a slit in it hung from a pack of wires, and the greased-up guy showed me I could stick a screwdriver in the slit and turn it just like a key. When he did, my little red baby roared right up. *Hot damn!* He kind of stood there, holding the screwdriver, gauging me. I had a sense he was expecting something. I pulled the sticky wad of bills from my apron–around thirty-eight bucks and well-worth it for his Jerry-rigged ignition fix–and held it up while giving him a sheepish will-this-do? kind of look.

"I 'ppreciate that," the black guy said, taking my wad of bills and sticking it quickly in the greased-rim pocket of his blue mechanic's pants. He handed me the screwdriver and said, "Now you get on out of here before the bossman comes back." We didn't hesitate. Dad shook the man's big hand, shoved me in the Escort, and slammed his hand twice on the top. Bam! Bam! That was my cue. *Let's go!* Dad jogged out to his Ram in the parking lot and we hightailed it (true story). For the next two years that I owned that car, I started it every time with that same thirty-eight dollar screwdriver which stayed always in the console between the seats. I didn't even have to lock the car when I got out because no one would know how to start it anyway. Car keys were a thing of the past for me! I never had to carry them. I'd get a real kick out of new folks who would get in the car with me for the first time and watch in amazement as I cranked her with the flathead. I'd laugh and tell them I had to use a Phillips head to open the trunk.

The real kicker, though, was when I sold that little red beauty to my buddy Bud–a fine upstanding American who slept, drank and smoked weed most of the day and worked at the Cracker Barrel most of the night. Every day–drink, smoke, repeat. But, he was a decent guy, trying to make his way. So when Bud found himself in need of a car, he and I made a handshake deal one night at the Barrel for the Escort. I handed the screwdriver over to him immediately but kept the title in my name while he paid me $200/week out of his tips until he'd forked over a sum total of $2,400 for the car–not bad considering that's what I'd paid for her four years prior. About a month into the deal, though, dependable Bud got himself pulled over one night for speeding. Thankfully he wasn't drinking too. When the state trooper shined the flashlight in the front seat and saw the mangled steering column, he thought Bud had stole the car–not much of a stretch seeing the state of the column and the fact that the car wasn't in his name. Somehow Bud talked the trooper into calling me so I could tell the cop our sad rent-to-own story and somehow it worked. I'm sure that story's been told a time or two around the state trooper's office. I don't think Bud ever got the ignition fixed either though. Why would he? Like I said, it was just easier–no keys, no hassle, no worry. I loved that car.

I couldn't help but think back on it as I sat on the boat the next morning, punching a flathead just like the one I used to use to start my old Escort, through the brim of a visor I had just picked up from the little boat supply store at the Clearwater Marina. Why was I punching a hole in a perfectly-good, brand-new hat? Because, as my dad would say, it needed some "modificating." I had already learned previously on this trip that, much like us, hats like to travel too. They feel the lightest breeze and they start to spread their little hat wings and threaten to leap right off your head out into the great windy unknown. This usually happens when you're topside and have your hands elbow-deep in the sails, tying something or holding onto something, or who knows what. Unfortunately the impulse to reach up and grab your hat in such a situation is so instinctive it's dangerous. Rather than sacrificing that stupid $8.49 visor from Walgreens to the Wind Gods, your dumb ass may reach up and grab it out of habit causing you to let go of something infinitely more important–like, I don't know, say a halyard or line or tool or perhaps your *one* hand-hold on the mast. I almost did it the day before when we were making our way into the Clearwater Pass, so I knew. Hats mustn't blow off.

So when it came time to replace that sacrificial visor, I wanted to find one with some kind of awesome tightening gadget or strap under the chin that would prevent it from blowing off–a chin-strap visor if you will. *Surely they sell those at a marina for sailboats,* I thought. *Surely.* Well, they don't. Or they do, but they're not visors. They're these safari-like western hats with this fancy "Tilley" name on them and they're eighty bucks. *No.* I'll pay an extra buck or two for a chin strap, but eighty? *No.* If the Malt-O-Meal background and screwdriver-start car hadn't made it clear enough, I might as well break the news to you: I'm cheap. Incredibly cheap. Sometimes embarrassingly cheap. Okay, not some times, most of the times. Now, was this habit developed mostly out of necessity while growing up, as my folks would say, paycheck-to-paycheck, saving up for college and then working two jobs all the way through? Of course. But, has it stuck well beyond its original need? Of course! And, I tend to think it's not in any way a bad quality for a scrimping, scraping sailor.

I used to shop at the thrift store all the time in college–still do on occasion, depending on what I'm looking for. I couldn't afford much else back then and the thrift store was a great place to find those plain blue and white button-down shirts you need as part of your "official" Cracker Barrel uniform. I picked up the necessary Cracker Barrel bottoms there too–those hot old lady khakis with the flattering pleats. Thirty-nine cents for a pair of pants? You betchya! But, my cheapness knew no bounds. If there was a fifty-cent pair that fit right, but a thirty-nine cent pair that just needed a little "modificating," I think you know which pair I would buy. I had a really unique way of tailoring these special pieces too–the snip, pull, staple, and glue method (patent pending). I invented the method when a snarly little manager at the Barrel tried to tell me once that he wasn't going to let me work the big-bucks Saturday night shift because my crappy thrift store pants had a tear near the ankle. Try to stiff me out of a $250 night? *No.* I grabbed a stapler from the host stand, ducked behind it, and stapled the tear right up–staples on the inside, even, so they wouldn't show. I showed him all was mended on the khaki front and started picking up tables before he could object. The staples held that night and for the next two years while I finished out my stint at the ol' Barrel. They also naturally became my favorite pair. Their little stapled seam acting as a badge of honor, a symbol of adversity overcome.

While stapling can work in certain circumstances, I eventually graduated to the glue–hot glue to be precise. That stuff works wonders on polyester. Sure the glue starts to show when you sit down and the material stretches but you just hide it. No problem. Keep your hand at your waist the entire time. *You can do that, Annie.* At least I didn't think it was a problem until I started wearing some of my one-hit hot-glue wonders to law firm interviews. Being the animated, arms-flailing type, I would often get to telling stories and would forget very quickly about my brilliant hand-waist-hide. I was soon baring my blotchy, glued seams to anyone who fancied to look. And trust me, they weren't hard to miss. Perhaps it was more than just my rough country edges and lewd jokes that resulted in the numerous polite declines. *Perhaps.*

While my frugal tendencies have dissipated some in my adult years, they've not been extinguished entirely. I still find it hard at times to buy expensive, well-made stuff that needs no modificating–not when I've got a hot glue gun waiting! The minute we started cruising on the boat–and I do mean the initial passage from Charlotte Harbor to Clearwater–I rigged up a handful of staple-and-glue type fixes that I thought would make our lives on the boat better. Some mortified Phillip to the core and I'm keeping a vow to him by not discussing them here. Others, however, that I'm proud to say were rigged up on this very first passage and have stuck to this day. A hook screw under the table, a small piece of five-fifty cord and a 3M adhesive hook secure the door to the head in the open position–which it remains 93.46% of the time. An eight-compartment duct tape creation still serves as our flashlights/tools/ sunscreen/sunglasses compartment under the companionway stairs. And a couple of nails and an elastic strap allow our trash can to fall open with the hatch door, just like them fancy ones in a high-end custom kitchen. Pretty bad ass staple-and-glue work, if you ask me, for a fraction of the store-bought cost. *You're welcome, Phillip.*

So, when it came to the necessary wind-resistant chin-strap upgrade I needed for the new visor, alas, I had to get creative again. I picked up a regular old "Clearwater Beach" visor at the marina shop that morning–thinking it would be fun to have my own memento from our eventful almost-crash with Lou, Red, and the gang. And it was well within the acceptable $8.49 vicinity. Then I started hacking into it. I cut two holes through the visor band on each side just in front of my ears and used the flathead screwdriver–seems that's a favorite tool of mine–to punch through and widen the holes so I could feed an elastic band into each hole of the visor and tie a knot on the inside. The fresh-cut ends also got a good burning to prevent further fraying. It may be cheap work but it's still a quality job. This resulted in my own make-shift elastic "chin-strap" that could sit freely on top of my head when I didn't need it, or that I could pull under my chin when I was heading into heavy winds. *Voila.* A chin-strap visor. Now I was ready to get back out there.

"Twenty to twenty-five knots," Phillip said as I finished rigging my

hat. In my short little sail career, I had at least picked up on some of the vernacular. I knew Phillip was talking about the wind, telling us how hard it was predicted to blow today out in the Gulf. A kettle of water was warming on the stove for coffee and we were piddling around in the cabin of the boat–doing what most sailors do in the morning, and the evening, and the afternoon–discussing the weather. "Seas still four to five, possibly six," Phillip added.

I knew he was talking about the sea state–the height of the waves–but the only word I could focus on was "still." *Still, still, still.* This was our second day to be stuck at a marina. Our second morning *not* making progress across the Gulf, but tied up *still* at a dock hundreds of miles from Pensacola. Phillip and I know now if it's blowing over twenty knots in the Gulf with waves greater than five feet, *still* is what you stay until it passes. And if it's still like that the next day, then you stay your happy little still ass at the dock and wait it out. That's what we know now, but then we were carrying with us on board one of the most dangerous things you can have on a sailboat–a schedule. We all had work weighing on us from home. Sitting there at the dock–with emails pouring in, calls going to voicemail, thinking of the four or five days we *still* had to travel to get back home and get a handle on those pressing needs–the need to leave felt urgent. After consulting with the *Bottom Line* guys and learning they were planning to head out that day, it seemed the right thing to do. At least if we left now, we would have another boat out there with us. If we waited until tomorrow and the conditions were still bad but we felt we still needed to leave, we would then be doing it alone. Having a buddy to make the passage with us tipped the scale. The boat was ready. The mattresses were in place. We were rested. So we decided it was time to go. The storm be damned! All we needed was a good breakfast before we got under sail.

We hit up the local greasy spoon for one last rendezvous with our sail groupies. With a sign that boasted a hearty tatted babe in a skimpy little sailor shirt stretched over huge bazoombas–I believe is the correct term–we were excited to check the place out. But it was a severely sad case of false advertising, because our waitress–the pile of toothpicks glued together that came walking up to our table–had no tats and certainly *no* bazoombas.

Now, was she a great waitress? Sure, of course. Excellent. The best. But, we didn't come there for good service. She had a captive audience, though, and she sold Phillip's mom several of the neon-

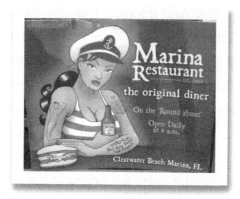

colored signature "Marina Restaurant" t-shirts that were hanging all over the walls. "All these are for sale," she said, with two syllables and a 'y.' "Sa-yull." Phillip's mom picked out a few and gave one to me as a good luck cruising gift as we were leaving. Phillip and I still call it my "big boobs t-shirt" as in memoriam. Unfortunately it suffered some serious stains on the Gulf Crossing and has now become my go-to top when we've got some greasy project we need to do on the boat. "Break out big boobs," Phillip will say. "We need to change the oil."

After the bazoomba breakfast we ran through one final round of readying on the boat and decided we were fit for travel. We checked in with the *Bottom Line* guys and they were ready to toss the dock lines and head out too. We picked a hailing channel to go to if we needed to talk via radio during the passage and mapped the course for our next stop—Apalachicola. It would be an approximate twenty-eight-hour passage (138 nautical miles) from Clearwater to Apalachicola—a pretty much straight shot across what I call the "armpit" of the Gulf. To be technical, I think it's the Big Bend, but armpit seems to get the point across a lot quicker. We headed out of the pass at Clearwater around 10:00 a.m. and had a great sail that morning.

The sun was just peeking through the clouds. We had some strong, but steady, northeast winds and we could see *Bottom Line* in the distance. The boat was performing beautifully. We felt like we had taken sufficient measures to ready her for the rough seas we knew we were going to face and we were ready to get the passage behind us. Everything was just peachy, until the squalls started to form on the horizon in the early afternoon. The waves were three to four at the time. We furled the Genny in a bit and pulled the main down to the first reef point so only about half of the sail was exposed to catch the wind. The *Bottom Line* guys had put some distance between us earlier in the day. We could no longer see them on the horizon but we knew we could hail them on the radio at anytime if we needed to check in. With the winds and seas increasing, we cranked the engine and started motor sailing. We were holding our heading, bracing for the storm.

The wind continued to build and was blowing a steady twenty-two knots by 3:00 p.m. with seas of four to five. I thought back to that seven-foot-wave image. Six was only a foot shorter than seven, and five was only one foot shorter than six. We weren't too far from that wretched "wall of water" image that had racked my brain the day before, when were still tied securely at the dock in Clearwater. The waves were also coming quickly, in short periods, giving us only a five-

or six-second break in between each one. By the time one of those monsters lulled the boat up and rolled underneath, it was just about time for another to hit us again. We rolled in the Genny completely and Mitch and I headed topside to bring the mainsail down entirely and lash her down. There were no smiles or "Atta girls" this time though as I pulled the sail ties from my shirt and handed one to Mitch to tie off. With the increased sea state, it was all we could do to focus and hold on while we wrestled the sail down. We were all business. I was part of the crew now, not some fragile "girlie" passenger. And I was needed. When the winds picked up, so did the waves and the rocking. Being on the boat in those conditions really did feel a lot like riding a horse. There's this big, strong, moving object beneath you that you are riding over the waves and rough terrain. All you can do is rock and sway and shift your weight with it to maintain balance. There's no controlling the movement of the boat. As a passenger, there is riding only.

Also with the course we were on heading to Apalachicola the swells were hitting us almost directly broadside on starboard, leaving us no way to turn into the waves to slice through. Instead, our boat rocked wildly to port as a wave lifted her up and then swung mightily back to starboard as the wave travelled under the boat and she slid down the backside of it. Port to starboard. Left to right–with startling pitch. We didn't have one of those instruments on our boat that tells you how far you are heeled over–a "tiltometer" I would call it, although I'm sure there is a more technical name–but we had to be swaying at least twenty, maybe twenty-five degrees to either side with every wave. Port to starboard. Left to right. Sometimes the water was just inches from the deck, lapping at the toerail as we leaned into the Gulf.

"Good bracing," Phillip had said to me, when we were shopping for boats. Time and again he told me we wanted, rather we *needed*, a cockpit that offered good bracing. *Bracing?* I had thought. *Jesus.* I akin bracing to seriously gripping for dear life–like bracing for a storm, bracing for an impact. *Is this the kind of "bracing" we would be doing in the cockpit of our boat?* When we had first sat in the cockpit of the Niagara back in Punta Gorda about a month prior, Phillip had sat on the bench of one side, put his feet up, easily reaching the bench seat on the other, and he pushed into it, allowing his back to wedge hard against the backing as he looked sternly at me. "Good bracing," he had said. I remembered sitting there next to him, matching his stern look and nodding, but not really having a clue why it was so important. Like a boy trying to learn how to fix an engine from his father, if he doesn't understand, he'll likely just nod and say "uh-huh." That's what

I'd done. *Uh-huh, Phillip. Good bracing. I'm with ya.* But, as I sat here now—the rain and waves spitting into the cockpit from all angles and the boat heeling harshly from left to right, left to right, my feet pressed up against the bench seat on the port side of the cockpit, my back wedged against the backing on starboard—I realized I was doing it instinctively, pushing hard on the bench seat across the cockpit when the boat heeled to port, and leaning hard into the backing when the boat heeled to starboard. I wasn't doing it out of comfort. I was doing it because it was necessary. *Good bracing*, I thought, as I rode up and over each horrendous wave with the coordinate effort of my feet and back alone.

My back was drenched, as was everyone's. The rain had started late in the afternoon and had spat at us now for hours. With the rain and waves splashing over the starboard deck we were all getting soaked in the cockpit. While we had each brought a jacket or two on the trip, it was clear they weren't standing up to the brutal conditions topside. I now know why they call it *foul* weather gear. But this weather was beyond foul. It was bitter, rotten—nasty even—in its delivery. Mitch and I had scoured the boat that afternoon hoping Jack had left some good foul weather gear behind—some serious offshore pieces—and boy did he! We struck gold with a complete Gorton's fisherman outfit—pants, jacket, boots, even a big yellow hat to complete the ensemble. Once we found and started swapping those out, a typical shift change between the three of us sounded something like this:

"Where's the Gorton pants?"

"I need the Gorton hat."

"Give me the Gorton boots!"

Phillip, Mitch, and I swapped and shared each piece of that yellow rubber suit during the wet stretch of the afternoon. When it came time to hold the helm, you could hear one of us holler at the other and barter for each piece. "Take the jacket this time and I'll keep the pants." "Give me the hat and you can keep the boots." I think I even heard at one point: "God, I love Gorton!" We certainly appreciated that dry, rubbery goodness. I do think it was one of the things that truly carried us through on that passage. *Thank you Jack!*

As we trudged on through the wet afternoon and the heeling continued, Mitch's condition and color continued to decline. Although he repeatedly denied our inquiries as to whether he was getting seasick, his skin was turning a lighter shade of grey every fifteen minutes. He kept fumbling around for something in his bag and couldn't find it. Watching Mitch struggle his way up and down the companionway stairs was like watching a grown man romping around the PlayPlace at McDonald's. While he tried to play it off—mumbling something about trying to find a flashlight or something as he would stumble down—he came up every time empty-handed, not even carrying a flashlight. After a little prodding, Mitch finally admitted to us—as if the ghoulish gray of his face hadn't revealed his dire status already—that he was looking for his Dramamine. I ransacked his bag for him and finally found it tucked away behind some hidden zipper in an outer pocket and he double-dosed.

Mitch bobbed around in the cockpit with us for another ten minutes or so—his head swimming on his shoulders—until he finally scrambled, turned around, and hurled violently over the back of the cockpit on the port side. There was no denying it now. Mitch was irretrievably seasick. While he did make it outside of the cockpit, at least, he hadn't made it outside of the *boat* and the pungent scent of vomit began to waft back in, making Phillip and I both swallow, try to breathe through our mouths, and question our own state of nausea. When Mitch finally finished, coughed a few times and turned back around to us–wiping his mouth with the back of his foul weather jacket–he looked ghastly. Phillip laid eyes on me. It seemed he was trying to discern without asking: "Are you okay? Are you going to be able to do this?" I hoped I conveyed back to him what I believed at the time: "I'm okay. I can do this."

All of this readying of the boat, the time we had spent lashing things down, tightening things, checking things, and the thought had never occurred to me that perhaps there should have been some readying of the crew. But, how do you prepare your mind and body for something like this–a violent, torrent passage at sea? Get a good night's sleep, eat a filling meal, take some Dramamine? Those things may help but they're not going to carry you. Outside of experience, you're either built to handle something like this out of the gate or you're not. As we beat around in the wet cockpit, I noticed my hand gripped tight on the corner of the dodger cover. Seeing the whites of my knuckles and the wet wadded-up bunch of green canvas in my hand took me back to a cold, rainy night in southern New Mexico, where I found myself just as uncomfortable, just as miserable, but just as determined. My mom, brother, stepdad and I were each sitting in a corner of our tiny square tent, gripping at the flimsy nylon trying to hold it down. A wicked storm had rolled in that afternoon and all through the night, the wind whipped at our tent, threatening to rip it from the stakes and send it sailing across the desert plateaus. Rain drove the sides of the tent inward, encroaching on what little soppy living space we had left in the center—our sleeping bags piled there in a muddy mess. There would be no sleeping in the tent that night. There would be no sleeping at all. I don't know whether it was the cost of the tent—which was ripping near the seams in our clenched fists anyway—or just the principle of the matter, but for whatever reason, my mom was not going to give in to that storm. "You hush and hold it!" she shouted to us, her voice cutting through the wind and rain with a fierceness that made us grip harder. Initially we held for her, but after a while we held for ourselves—if for nothing more than to spite her. *Fuck you storm!* We weren't giving in either.

"Hold on," Phillip shouted, jolting me back, as a big, black wall of water made its way toward the boat. "Hold on," he said again for good measure. The swell seemed to reach under the boat, grab her keel and tilt her over from below. She groaned and screamed back at the vast blackness engulfing her, gripped the wave in retaliation and heeled mightily over it. The motion of the boat sliding down the backside of the wave threw me against the bench seat in the cockpit with alarming force, reminding me for the second time in my life how incredibly inconsequential we are to Mother Nature—how little we weigh, how little we are, how little we *matter*. It was a similar, sickening smack onto the thick clay mud of the farm in Alabama that had reminded me the first time. A hurricane was threatening to rip through our pastures and my dad and I had spent the afternoon in slanting sheets of rain drilling holes in the tin roof of the barn and running cable wire down to long rebar stakes we'd hammered into the ground in hopes they would hold the roof down in the expected sixty miles-per-hour winds. At one point in the night it was my dad, his ranch-hand Danny, and I out there holding some of the cables ourselves. I had wrapped a cable around my midsection at one point and laid all of my weight down on it in the thick orange clay–using the sum total of me and all the force I could possibly exert–to battle the storm. As if in mockery of my meager efforts, the wind peeled back that tin roof several times just enough to lift my ragged body off of the ground and slam it back down in the mud. It seemed she was having fun dangling us like puppets.

Conditions like that and like the ones we were facing out in the open Gulf make you realize how powerless you really are. A thousand similar wet, windy images flashed through my mind as I continued to brace myself in the cockpit. I was thankful at the time to have survived each of those vicious encounters with nature and I found myself thankful for them now as well, because they had certainly helped to ready me for the state we were currently in. I hoped they had also readied me for what was to come. We were way out in the Gulf of Mexico–hundreds of miles from civilization, safety, the shore–and hundreds of miles above the black, buried bottom. There was no pulling off of the road or pulling into a rest stop for cover. No saying "fuck this tent," or "fuck this roof," and going back to the car or house for shelter. We were the tent. We were the roof. *We* were the flailing, ripping thing at the complete and utter and mercy of the storm. There was no way out of this.

Neither Phillip nor I said a word as the boat continued to pitch and sway and sheets of water splattered into the cockpit–thankfully washing away the remnants and stench of Mitch's vomit. Phillip was at the helm, had been all day, and Mitch now sat on the port side–his head dangling and bobbing against his chest with the waves. At least knew one thing was clear. I wasn't prone to seasickness. That meant I was still upright and coherent, which also meant I was all Phillip had. I would have to do–a Loctite-tough, bull rider's daughter. It was Phillip and me, the Captain and I, and the six-foot waves that came every four to six seconds. It was hour four of thirty.

TWELVE

Non-Drowsy My Ass

"It's out," Phillip said as he banged it against the heel of his palm a few times. I watched as he fiddled with it and banged it a few more times, hoping it would miraculously turn back on, start whirring and buzzing and a scratchy voice would come over saying "Hey you guys. Yeah, you, the idiots crossing the Gulf alone. You guys alright?" But, it didn't. It just sat there–all dead-like, just as Phillip had diagnosed. Even Mitch swayed his head into upright position and watched Phillip with visible worry.

"It's … " Phillip started but paused, whacking it one more time or two before giving up, "it's just out." He finally resolved and put it back on its wet clip on the stern rail. It sat there useless, swaying from side to side with the heeling of the boat. *It* was the radio–the handheld that we kept in the cockpit, our means of communication with the nearby marine world, our hailing mechanism, our string-and-can to the only other vessel we knew that was out there with us–the *Bottom Line* guys–and it was out. We were 150 miles from shore in the churning

Gulf and we were incommunicado, out of range, out of reach, off the grid.

Phillip asked me to take over for a bit so he could check the main unit down below and see if he could splice together some meager connection to the outside world. It was the first time I had held the wheel in those conditions. But with Mitch sitting slumped in the corner of the cockpit, in reach of the bucket I had designated for him and secured in the sink, I was the only option. Phillip gave me one solemn look before he headed down the companionway stairs, inquiring without actually asking: "You got it?" I nodded back at him, trying to convey what I thought was unquestionable courage. *Of course, I've got this. Done it a hundred times.* I finished the thought jokingly to myself. *Go ahead, go on down. Take your time. Make a sandwich. Leave me up here, at the helm of this massive boat in the middle of this raging storm. No problem. Fuhgeddaboudit,* I said to myself all DeNiro-like. And then he did. Phillip went down. He left me up there and forgot all about it. When he was out of sight I swallowed and looked out and willed myself to focus. I knew our heading. I knew what I needed to hold. I knew to look out for some of the larger, rogue waves, to warn Phillip to hold tight if I saw one, and to try and slice through those as best I could. I knew the wind direction and I knew which ways *not* to turn the boat in order to keep the sails full. *You've got this,* I told myself. Then I tried desperately to believe it. I was mesmerized at first by the true power of the waves, their ability to lift and drop the boat with each passing peak. It was much more pronounced sitting behind the wheel–in actual control of the boat–than just sitting on the bench seat of the cockpit and it was hard for me to believe every time the boat leaned over that it was, in fact, going to right itself.

"You doing alright up there?" Phillip hollered up after a minute or two while he continued to tinker with the radio down below. And while I wanted to say, "Yes. Just fine. Everything's great. I've got this," the first thing that came tumbling uncontrollably out of my mouth was the single threatening thought I couldn't shake.

"If you *tell me*," I shouted as the boat heeled violently to port, "it's not going to *tip over*," as the boat heeled violently back to starboard, "I'll believe you!"

"It's not going to tip over." He said it calmly, slowly, with resolve. And I said it again to myself just to reinforce it. *It's not going to tip over.*

And, it didn't. Every time a wave would grab us on the starboard side and heel us over, the boat would hold fast, cling to the water, and climb with startling agility over the crest of the wave only to come sliding down the back side. She heeled and climbed and swayed but she never tipped over. Instead she popped right back up. Every time. The boat always came back up. She was like a weeble wobble. After enough heeling and righting, heeling and righting, I worried about it no more. I started to develop limitless trust in the boat. No matter how far she heeled over, I never believed for one second that she would actually *tip* over. Not ever. It was as if the keel somehow reached deep every time a wave came, grabbed something down in the depths of the murky water and held on with unshakeable strength until the wave passed under. I was thoroughly impressed with the boat's weeble capabilities.

"Everything's fine. I've got it," I shouted back down to Phillip when he checked on me again after a few minutes. And I did. Have it. At least I felt like I did. Holding the helm was difficult but well within the range of my capabilities at the moment. Even here, on my first real passage at sea—or in the Gulf, same difference—it was shocking how much the heading would shift with each passing wave. Heading north, northwest toward Apalachicola, we were holding a heading of about 315 degree or so, but it was more of an average than a constant. When the boat climbed a massive wave on the starboard side, the needle on the compass would swing down to the low 300's. Then when the wave passed under and the boat rocked over to starboard, the needle would fall back the other way to the upper 320's. All you could do was try to hold some average between the two to keep the boat roughly on course. I was "holding our heading" as best as I could, but it felt more like zig-zagging it—weaving in and out of it, like pole bending in the rodeo. In and out, in and out.

While it was certainly do-able—here I was *doing* it—it was still incredibly tiring and worrisome. I was in control of the boat. I was steering it across a huge body of angry water. What if I was the one holding the helm when something tragic happened—we hit that whale or rogue iceberg I had imagined when all we were doing was imagining this adventure. I was so eager for Phillip to come back to relieve me but I knew he was working on something almost as important as the holding of our heading at the moment, which was the 'fixing of our radio' if that was even possible. So I held it. I stayed. I squinted at the compass and watched the needle swing back and forth and I clutched the wheel trying to keep the needle within a manageable range. 305 to

318. 309 to 322. *Steady girl.* Without even realizing it, I had propped one foot up on the bench on the port side of the cockpit and was bracing myself just as Phillip had when he was steering. As wet and miserable as we were, I knew the cockpit was cocooning and sheltering us more than we realized. It was really the boat who was bracing each time another wave struck, preparing to climb and descend it to keep us safe. We were riding safely in the saddle. I started to feel secure and confident–comfortable, almost–at the helm, but it seemed confidence was my Achilles heel on this trip because there it went again.

"Ping!"

Another bolt head shooting off to its watery grave in the cockpit floor. *Shit!* I thought, then "Shit!" I said. Of course this happens when I'm holding the helm. *Of-fucking-course.* Phillip had heard it from down below. He immediately stuck his head through the companionway. Even Mitch roused for a moment out of his sickness-slumber in the corner and started looking groggily around the cockpit floor. He already knew it, but he couldn't help asking, "Was that another?"

While I did not yet have any confirmation of what exactly had "pinged" while, once again, I was handling something on the boat–this time the helm–I knew it too. "I'm sure it was," I told him, my shoulders already up in an apologetic shrug. I hate to say it, but with all of the commotion and chaos of trying to set up the storm sail, checking on the dinghy and the outboard, conferring with Jack about readying the boat, and actually being out here now in the wicked storm we had been ceremoniously readying ourselves for, we had forgot all about it. That damn bolt–or bolt *head*, rather–the first one that had sheared through and pinged just as this one had when we were making our way to Clearwater. How could we have forgotten? It was a crazy couple of days, that's how. But we certainly remembered now. *Now* that bolt was the most important item on the agenda, so Phillip immediately switched gears.

"Well, the radio's out. I don't know why," he said as he made his way up to the helm. "Let me take the wheel. You find the bolt."

Phillip was so decisive on that trip. The more I look back on it, the more it impresses me. There was never hesitation. I can't say that he made all the right calls, but at least he made them quickly and spent no time questioning them. I guess with the crew and conditions at hand, he had no other choice. But that doesn't always enable people to do what is necessary. We moved from one problem to the next.

The death of the radio was actually softened by the loss of Bolt No. 2. *Radio? Who gives a crap about the radio? We've got bolts shearing here.* I dropped to my knees in the cockpit floor and started looking for what we were sure was going to be another bolt head, sheared off much like the other. And we were right. I found it within a minute and compared it to the other we had put in the companionway tray, which houses the kind of items you would typically find in the "junk drawer" in a kitchen—nail clippers, flashlights, common tools and, now, sheared bolt heads all go in the tray. The two were the same. We all started looking around the cockpit—at shackles and pulleys, the bimini frame—for some kind of clue, but it seemed the boat didn't have time to sit around and wait for us to find it. She screamed at us in her suffering—a high-pitched screech that rang out from behind Phillip at the wheel. We had heard a similar sound all afternoon, but it had been lower-pitched, far more muffled, not nearly as desperate. It had squeaked out each time the boat heeled to port, along with many other sounds that squeaked out with each heel, to both port and starboard. But, now it was pronounced. It was no longer a squeak. It was a painful wail. It was the dinghy.

Davits that had once held her steady behind the boat now had a range of motion and were allowing the dinghy to swing a good ten inches either way and bang to port each time a wave shoved the boat over. We watched in silence as the davit arms swayed a little to the right when the boat slid down a wave and then, in horror, as the davit arms swung around swiftly to port when the next wave came and tipped the boat over. The weight of the dinghy with the outboard leading the way would come sailing down and bang with a sickening thud when the davits reached their limit. Wave, heel, clang. Wave, heel, *clang*. The davit arms were actually swinging from side to side, visibly, with each passing wave. I made my way toward the bracket that held the davits to the stern rail on the port side—almost afraid of what I would find. And sure enough, two bolts were missing from the bracket. Barren little holes were left behind where Bolt No. 1 and Bolt No. 2 had once been nestled. I could even see a little scrape and discoloration on the stern rail where the bracket had scooted over about a half inch to port with all of the swinging and banging. The entire set-up on the back—the davits, the brackets, the dinghy with the outboard, all of it—was inching its way slowly over to port. Brackets that had once been closed tightly together with four bolts were now stretched apart with a visible gap in between that widened with each crashing bang of the davits to port. There was no way Loctite would fix this. But something had to.

We all started to throw out different options. Even Mitch perked up and offered a few. Put another bolt in there, tie the dinghy over to starboard, is there any way to get the outboard off now? We all knew there wasn't. Not in this sea state, but you ask anyway. Words you hope can be true topple out of your mouth uncontrollably. We knew though that we had to secure her. The bracket on the port side was stretching further open with each clang to port. Mitch and I went on a hunt for bolts, nuts, cotter pins, anything we could put in the bracket to tighten it back together. We found a couple of bolts that fit through, but they were not quite the right size and–even if they were–there was no way to fight the wind, waves and periodic weight of the crashing dinghy in order to tighten a nut down on the back side. We had brought a lot of spare parts for the passage—primary and secondary fuel filters, oil filters, impellers, gaskets, fuses, belts, you name it. We felt we had really tried to think of everything that could possibly go wrong but I have to say, replacement bolts for the dinghy davits just in case they started *shearing* through was not something we had planned for. We got creative. We started filling the bolt holes with cotter pins for sails, allen wrenches, anything that would slide through and somewhat hold. But, within fifteen minutes of banging, each of these would either fall out or shear through as well, landing with another sickening ping in the cockpit. A litany of slain bolt soldiers littered the floor.

We started tying the dinghy with any rope available, trying to stop it from banging to port every time we climbed a wave. We tied three spare lines from the davit arm on the starboard side down to the starboard rail and cleat, which helped some, but it's hard to stop 150 free pounds from banging around on the stern rail once the brackets have been compromised. It was like we had a baby elephant strung up back there.

There was just so much weight and force to try and counterbalance. Wave, heel, clang. Wave, heel, *clang.* The seas were relentless—each time hitting with blunt force on the starboard side and each time causing the davit arms to swing around to port and the dinghy to bang. I swear it felt like the seas were *trying* to knock the dinghy off, like it was a fun carnival game or something. We tied one last thick line on the dinghy and sat back for a minute. Mitch had really stepped up to the plate forcing himself to lean over and around, up and down, swaying left

and right wrestling the dinghy like that, when we all knew he was sick as a dog. I heard him sputter and retch a few times—while we were hard at it tying the dinghy—but he didn't complain. When we finally sat back in the cockpit for a spell to see what kind of effect our efforts had had on that damn dinghy, it was clear he was done.

That was the last physical act he could stomach. I watched as Mitch's head dropped to his chest and he swallowed back something I don't even want to imagine. I would have patted him on the shoulder and told him what a great job he'd been doing but I was too busy taking his picture. I mean, he was seasick. He wasn't dying. It was clear, though, he needed a break.

"Holler if you need me," he mumbled as he hobbled down the stairs. No apologies were included but none were needed. He had been there when it counted and we knew he would rise as best he could

to the occasion again, if the occasion called. Now, what that occasion might *be* exactly? I wasn't sure. We weren't in immediate danger, but with the steady four- to six-foot waves hitting us broadside, the banging dinghy, and the lack of radio, we weren't doing real swell either. There was nothing more to do at the moment other than hold the helm, so we let him rest. I heard Mitch grab his spit bucket from the sink, hit the settee with a thud and, within minutes, he was out. His Dramamine must have finally kicked in.

And he laid like that–lifeless–for hours. Phillip said he had never seen someone so seasick able to sleep so damn well. I had to laugh when I went down later to get some water and snacks for Phillip and me in the cockpit and saw Mitch's half-smashed box of Dramamine on the floor. *Non-drowsy* it said. "Non-drowsy my ass," I said back in the cockpit as I watched Mitch continue to take in deep, husky draws and blow them out in big, breathy huffs. He lumbered like an old tree sloth. Phillip and I ate granola bars and Cheezits for dinner, switching shifts at the helm while steady winds of twenty to twenty-two knots continued to howl over the boat and the constant, *constant* waves smacked her on the starboard side. Port to starboard. Left to right. For hours. Thick, choking clouds had caked the sky all day. But as we ate one lone streak of sunlight pierced through on the horizon only to grace us for a moment before dipping down below the black sea.

Darkness then set in around us. The wind screamed as it passed over the mast and through the cockpit. It was blowing so hard it stung our eyes and made it hard to keep them open, particularly in light of the rain–which, without the wind, was only a steady dusting–but the gusts transformed it into pelting sheets. The sound of the waves against the hull and the groaning and creaking of the boat as she tipped mightily over each wave became far more prevalent, almost haunting, at night. As if our sense of sound was heightened. Think how much easier it is to hear a door creak in a pitch black room when sound

seems like your only sense. The darkness amplified everything. After a couple more hours of heavy heeling, the clanging of the dinghy was no longer a painful wail but a shrill scream in the dark. Every time she came slamming down to port, the davits would swing around and shriek in pain when the dinghy came crashing down.

Phillip and I started walking through the various alternatives. There was no way we could pull all 150 pounds of her up out of the water and onto the deck in four- to six-foot waves. She would either make it to shore on broke-down davits or she would have to be sacrificed at sea. We didn't want to have to cut the dinghy off. No one would. It was an awesome dinghy–a Caribe, six-seater, rigid inflatable with a rare two-stroke fifteen-horsepower outboard on it, the one our broker had been "really excited about" when we were boat shopping. But as Phillip explained to me, if the davits completely failed and the dinghy hit the water, there was a chance she could pull the sailboat

down with her—perhaps tipping it enough to cause water to come in or, worst case scenario, causing the boat to tip over entirely. There was also the possibility that the pull of the dinghy in the water could rip the stern rail right off the boat, leaving a gaping hole in the deck that would allow water to come in.

"As soon as she hits, we've got to cut her off as fast as possible," Phillip said. I have to admit when the dinghy first started banging and the davits bolts started shearing, I knew it wasn't a good thing but I had no idea the potential danger it could cause. A hole in the boat? The boat tipping over? The boat sinking? *Holy shit!* If we had to cut off a finger to save the hand, so be it. I trusted Phillip wholeheartedly with the decision. If he said cut it off, I would cut it off.

I wasn't frightened so much as I was worried for the boat. It's a fear that, to this day, still trumps any thoughts of my own safety. When we find ourselves in unfavorable conditions, strong winds, heavy seas, difficult docking, I worry incessantly about that boat. I hate to see her under strain, in duress, suffering, bending, groaning, creaking, any of the like. I also hate to see Phillip worry about the boat. It's his absolute favorite thing. It's what we've worked so hard for. It's our ticket to world travel. And, here she was, crying out from the clawing dinghy on her back, begging us to help her. "Make it stop," she screamed. "Do something!"

When the last and final "ping" rang out, it pierced the night like a shrill animal cry in the jungle. Phillip and I heard the bolt zip overhead and hit the cockpit floor with a sad clatter. Bolt No. 3. Another soldier down. The next time the boat heeled over to port the shriek of the davits was undeniable. We were not going to be able to save her. I inspected the stern rail and could see the brackets had now worked their way over another inch to port and were scooching now each time–visibly–with the slam of the dinghy on the left side. This was it. It was happening.

A resolve came over Phillip. He took his eyes off of the davits, turned to face forward in the cockpit and spoke to me in short, commanding sentences in a tone I had never heard from him before.

"We need to get ready to cut it off. Go wake Mitch."

THIRTEEN

I'm Getting Sparks

"This?" I asked as I held it up for Mitch to see. It was a hacksaw. A real live, no-shit hacksaw. I couldn't believe the things that were running through my mind. *Will this cut through the rope? What about scissors? No. Scissors won't do. A steak knife? No. Too dangerous. Dangerous?* The thought was laughable now. Everything was dangerous. Crossing the Gulf in a sailboat is dangerous. Doing it in four- to six-foot seas is more dangerous. Cutting a dinghy off the back of the boat is dangerous. Doing it in four- to six-foot seas is more dangerous. But doing it with a steak knife? I honestly didn't know what impact that would have on the danger level at that point. We were going to have to do it. While anything with a blade would work, the sharper the instrument the *safer* it would actually be. So my weapon of choice? The hacksaw. Mitch chose a dive knife—a big one. It looked like that one Crocodile Dundee always carried around. Even in the midst of our scurrying, it still made me think of the scene where some small-timing, small-town biker bully pulls a little street knife on Dundee. "That's not a knife," Dundee says as he pulls out his huge, pirate-shaped foot-long knife and waves it in their face. "That's a knife." I had a hacksaw and what Mitch had was certainly the Dundee-equivalent for a knife. In addition to those, he and I also put together a small array of various other cutting mechanisms—a steak knife, a box cutter and a secondary, less Dundee-like dive knife—in case one went overboard or in case Phillip needed to jump up and help us cut or, perhaps, in case Mitch and I needed to cut two-handed, like Samurais. *Whuh-chaw!* We had no idea what all of the possible "in cases" were but we were hoping we'd be ready.

To Mitch's credit, he had woke without hesitation when I shook him to and told him we needed him. It was around 11:00 p.m. He'd been sleeping for about seven hours. But, the minute I said, "The dinghy's about to go," he had sat up, shook off the nausea, and snapped into action. We now had all of our cutting devices laid out on a towel in the cockpit like a surgical tray for Phillip—as if it would proceed like some formal operation. *Scalpel.* We knew it wouldn't. This was going to be chaos—utter and complete chaos. The boat was still heeling heavily with each wave. Port to starboard. Left to right. The cockpit was wet and slippery. And we were now in the dark, in the churning depths of the Gulf, without a radio, and we were about to hang over the stern rail and cut our only life raft off of the boat in five-foot waves. Nothing formal or orderly was about to occur.

I'm not sure whether Mitch was too sick to speak or just didn't feel there was anything to add, but he sat silently next to me on the cockpit bench facing the stern. We were both watching the dinghy behind Phillip as she clanged around the final few times to port—the davit brackets scooching further along the rail to port with each bang. I clenched the hacksaw in my hand and tested my flashlight to make sure it fit well in my teeth. I knew I was going to need two hands for the cutting and bracing, so the mouth was the last option for holding a flashlight. *Light. Saw. Check.* I have to admit the thought of falling overboard during the process had not yet crossed my mind. A slip and a slice of the hand had and I saw it with startling clarity—a quick slit into the meat of my finger, so fast and deep it took the blood a second to fill the paper thin sliver and come pouring out. I *had* thought of that. But falling over into the raging black abyss? *Nope. Not yet.* I gave Mitch the headlamp and he was fastening it on his head—the dive knife still in the hand he was using to pull the band down on the back of his head—when the dinghy hit.

A huge swell tipped us to port and when the dinghy came swinging around the davits finally gave up. They broke off the stern rail with a thunderous rip as the dinghy crashed into the water, outboard first. The boat groaned and pulled hard to her port side. As big and lumbering and heavy as our boat felt at times, it amazed me now to see how sensitive she could be. The weight of the dinghy dragging in the water pulled hard on her and buried the toerail on the port side. It was like we were pulling an anchor. The dinghy foamed and flailed in the water like a panicked drowning victim and the cockpit filled with the smell of oil and fuel. The outboard was submerged—choking on waves and water—and leaking fluids everywhere. That was the first time I had ever thought about the gas. While I had understood what Phillip told me earlier about the dangers we faced once the dinghy hit the water, understanding them was different than actually feeling them, experiencing them, *smelling* them in real time.

"Cut if off!" Phillip shouted. His voice charging through the wind and waves and clanging of the dinghy.

Mitch grabbed his knife, I grabbed my hacksaw, and we started attacking the lines. All of that tying and retying we had done earlier to try and keep the dinghy from swinging was now working against us. There were lines upon lines–some running out to the dinghy, back to the boat, others from the boat out to the dinghy and back again–and they were now all tangled up in between. There was no time to try and untie or salvage them. The lines were an easy casualty to save the boat. Mitch and I cut with fury. It was dark behind the boat though and we were struggling to see the lines and, worse, distinguish them from our own–or worse still, one another's–hands and fingers. I had a flashlight clenched tight in my teeth, but its beam was still bouncing and bobbing with every wave. We were also having trouble reaching the lines. Once the dinghy hit the water, they were a good three or four feet from the back of the boat. Mitch is a tall guy, but his height could only take him so far standing on the stern. One of us had to scale the stern rail and reach out. I gave Mitch my flashlight, sent him to the high side of the cockpit, and told him to hold the light for me. He didn't question me once. He just did it. We were all acting on our own internal chains of command–instructing and obeying in the same breath.

I climbed over the stern rail on the port side and hooked one foot back in the cockpit so I could reach out to the end of the davits. Despite the water and wind attacking us, gas still permeated the air.

The dinghy kicked and flailed at the end of the lines–like a rabid dog on a leash, salivating and snapping at us in rebellion–like she knew we were sacrificing her. Reaching my hands out to the lines, I almost felt like they were going to get bit. Mitch held the light steady on a clean point so I could see to saw through it. I gripped the line in my left hand and started sawing with the right, trying not to use the line for balance so I wouldn't fall the minute I cut through it. I was watching my hands cut–back and forth, back and forth–but I felt like I could almost see us from above too, standing out in the Gulf looking at the boat. Phillip is holding the wheel, trying to keep the boat balanced, steering to starboard as much as possible. He keeps turning to check on Mitch and me but says nothing, knowing we're sawing and cutting and working as hard as we can. Mitch is gripping the rail on the starboard side, one foot wedged against the cockpit seat–his sick, sad body bouncing with every wave–but he's holding a steady beam of light on me. And me. I'm extended out, my entire body length off the back of the boat, one lone foot reaching back to a rail, gritting my teeth and squinting into the rain while I saw through the line. I was there, doing it, but I felt like I could see it from afar at the same time. It was surreal. We looked like a living episode of *Deadliest Catch*–like we all should have tattoos and shout in thick Irish accents. We were like Hook-mouth! That weathered, scarred, rusty old salt I had watched on my very first sail, as he leapt topside and brought the mainsail down. We were like him!

"She needs to go!" Phillip hollered into the wind. The more lines I cut, the more the dinghy made contact with the water and pulled us further over to port. The boat couldn't tolerate much more pull to port. We didn't respond. It was clear he was right. She needed to go. I made my way up to the high side to cut the last of the lines on the starboard side, Mitch still lighting my way. The last line I grabbed felt particularly tough. When I first struck it with the saw, it sparked. I pulled back–momentarily frozen–frightened, smelling the gas fumes that were still emanating from the outboard motor, stopping purely out of instinct.

"I'm getting sparks!" I shouted to Phillip. It was the first thing I'd said to him since the dinghy hit. He reached back and felt the "line" I was holding. It was the cord to the navigation light that was mounted on the davits, like brake lights behind a trailer. I followed it down and could see the nav light dimly lit, flickering and choking behind the boat. It wasn't a line. It was a cord to a light. It was an electrical cord and it sparked.

"Cut it," Phillip said.

Cut it, he said. So, cut it I did. I bit my teeth together as hard as I could thinking I had heard some story somewhere where someone–when he got shocked–had bit right through his tongue because it was between his teeth at the time. Don't ask me who this someone was, when I heard about him and his tongue, or if it's even true, and how I was able to conjure that right before I was about to do something that might shock me, because I can't tell you. It just popped into my mind. I clenched my teeth–tongue inside–gripped the cord with one hand, and started sawing with the other. It sparked. It sheared. It finally ripped in two and I didn't get shocked or blown up. That wretched cord was the last surly line holding the dinghy on. When the hacksaw made it through the final inch of rubber and wire, the dinghy crashed into the water and finally began to pull away from the boat. Mitch and I were just about to lean back and breathe for the first time when Phillip's voice broke through.

"Get the lines in," he shouted. Again it was a short, direct instruction that immediately hit its intended target. Frayed, mangled lines were dragging helplessly from the back of the boat. Lines that we had just spent the last ten minutes cutting, shearing and ripping off the dinghy were now sinking into the water, threatening to choke our propeller. Thankfully Phillip had the wherewithal to still think clearly in that moment and focus on what mattered. Mitch and I didn't take a breath. We popped right back up, snapped to attention and started grabbing lines viciously and throwing them into the cockpit with reckless abandon. We hit Phillip with several of them–big wet knots flogging him–but he didn't say a word. He hunkered down, held the wheel, and steadied the boat while Mitch and I heaved the last of them in.

Afterward we all fell into a heap in the cockpit, drenched and shaken, but feeling more alive in that moment than we had the entire trip. I doubt Mitch could even comprehend nausea at that moment. Our bodies were feasting on adrenaline. We sat there–our chests heaving in unison it seemed–gathering our thoughts and wondering if what just happened had *really* happened. Phillip shined a light out into the sea as it to confirm our collective inquiry and there it was. The dinghy. About fifty yards away from the boat, lines floating around her like spindly fingers reaching back for us. She was truly out there—detached from the boat and floating away. We had really done it. Cut her off. The damn dinghy. The boat breathed a sigh of relief as if she had just finished a forty-mile march and finally set her rucksack down to air her sweaty back. Her heeling back and forth was now graceful–soothing almost–and we all finally appreciated how much she had been struggling with the dinghy on her back. We breathed with her–equally relieved–but our faces were still heavy with worry. We were hundreds of miles from shore, slugging across the black waters of the Gulf, in the middle of the night, without a radio, and now,without a dinghy. And we were only half-way there.

FOURTEEN

Right of the River

When my brother and I were kids we used to play at the drain pipes. That's what we called them anyway. They were these huge concrete culverts back in Clovis, New Mexico that drained rainwater into the town's murky little inner-city lake—if you can call it that. It was really more of a muck pond for the city's drainage. There were three pipes at the beginning—the center one standing probably twelve feet in diameter—stretching way above our little-kid heads at the entrance, but it got smaller the deeper you walked in. It continued to shrink all the way to the end, where the pipes drained into the north corner of the muck pond. At the end, the pipes were only three-or-so feet in diameter—still plenty big enough for us scrawny youngsters to make our way out—but no one was really sure whether it was big enough all the way to the end. Well no one except Ronnie Manfree, the only kid at Highland Elementary who had allegedly made it all the way through. Two fifth grade boys claimed to have witnessed Ronnie's muddy exit at the lake on summer and it became school legend. They say Ronnie initially had a buddy on the famous trek but that he bailed out about

halfway through and ran back, leaving Ronnie to push forward alone and making him even more legendary.

That happened a lot though. Most kids could make it past the first turn in the pipe–*just* past it–but then they screamed, turned, and hightailed it back. Tons of kids did that. But the real test came after the second turn. If you continued to tiptoe forward after the *second* turn you had some real guts. The continual shrinkage of the pipe worried us some, as well as a flash flood and the gunky residue on the bottom. We thought it might get deeper and nastier the further you went until your feet sank in it, leaving you stuck in the pipe forever. These were all legitimate concerns for nine-year-olds. But, the true fear factor in the pipes was the dark. The first hundred yards or so of the pipe was lit by the sun. Once you completed the first turn–it was to the left, I'll never forget–the second leg of the pipe, which was a longer two or three hundred yards, was dark moving forward but still lit behind by a single streak of light from the first leg. So, even though you were moving forward in the dark, you could always turn around, see the streak of light, and know you still had an exit you could run toward if one of those salivating, fanged pipe monsters–that we all imagined–appeared ahead in your flashlight beam. After you rounded the *second* turn, though–it was to the right, I'll never forget that either–that's when the real fear set in.

After the second turn, there was no streak of light behind you. There was no light in front of you, no light anywhere, nothing guiding your path to safety. It was utter and complete darkness, backward and forward. It's been a rare occasion that I've found myself encompassed again in that degree of darkness. In the pipes, the darkness is engulfing, capable of swallowing you whole, to where you can't see your own hand right in front of your face. I would wave and wiggle mine right in front of my face to see if I could sense it from the air disturbance alone. I would tell myself when *I* was doing the wiggling that I could but when we tested the theory–waving and wiggling our hands in front of each others' faces–it became clear we could not. In the pipes anything could occur right in front of our faces and we wouldn't know. That slimy pipe monster could play a game of Eenie Meenie Miney Moe–pointing his filthy, razor-sharp claws at each of our noses, deciding which one of us he was going to eat first–and we wouldn't know.

The pipes also reverberated sound so that you couldn't tell which direction it came from. If one of us brats in a small pack decided after the first turn that it was too much, we couldn't handle it, we just *had* to run, the sequence usually started with a shrill scream that roared through the pipe seemingly coming from every direction–the scariest being from the black abyss in front of you. You tried to tell yourself it was just Wet-His-Pants Willie in the back of your pack who had screamed but there was always the fear that the scream had actually come from some lost kid who'd been stuck in the pipes for weeks–making his way, finally, out from the depths, with a charging pipe monster behind him. No one wanted to stick around to be sure. Once one kid started screaming and running, the whole lot of us would usually start running as well, and screaming too. You couldn't help it.

The only way we knew to hold fast during a scream retreat was to have a buddy, someone whom you had made a pact with before you walked into the tunnel–promising one another that you would stay together, no matter what happened, and keep moving forward together toward your shaky beam of flashlight in the dark. If Willie screamed and started running, you would grab your buddy, hold your position, hold hands if you needed to (no one talked about it afterward), and wait for the roar of shouts and footsteps to calm before you breathed it off, picked back up again and kept moving forward. A buddy was a must in the pipes, second only to a good flashlight.

As we sat now in the cockpit of the boat–still heeling to and fro with every wave–I felt like we'd just made that second turn in the pipes. After a few minutes I clicked my flashlight on and looked out at the water behind us and could no longer see the dinghy, only darkness. She'd been swallowed whole by the black churning water. We were surrounded entirely by the black churning water. Now with no lit exit behind us *and* no buddy. There would be no screaming and running toward the light, no fleeing from the slobbering pipe monster, no retreat. We'd made it too far to go any way but forward, into the dark, toward Apalachicola. That was the only option.

Mitch heaved and swallowed and scrambled for his bucket—thankfully grabbing it in time—but little came of it. I started to wonder how he had made it through that entire dinghy incident without retching but then I realized he probably didn't have much left to offer at that point, which was probably worse. He hobbled down below, again without a word and without apology as none was needed. Mitch had done his job and he could barely hold his head up. We let him go. His "non-drowsy" Dramamine kicked right back in, though, and he slept another eight-or-so hours until we woke him later the next morning. *Non-drowsy, my ass.* Phillip and I stayed up at the helm through the night—taking shifts, eating crackers, and mostly sitting in silence. While the heeling of the boat was still pronounced, without the clanging dinghy banging around off-balance on the back, it was now smooth—pleasant almost—like a gentle amusement park ride. Without the cumbersome dinghy, the boat was so agile, so graceful. What had once felt about as pleasant as the dragging of heavy metal hooks and tires across sheet metal now felt like a summer afternoon on a sun-drenched porch swing. Don't get me wrong, it was still spitting rain and we were chilled and soaked, clinging to the helm like a wet cat on the edge of the tub. But without the screeching of the dinghy, it was infinitely better. I curled up next to Phillip at the helm, laid my head on his back, closed my eyes and let the movement and sounds of the boat seep in. Although serene, the night was a bit eerie in the sense that we could not, had not, seen the horizon since sunset and there was no sign of any other vessel out in the Gulf that night—no other ship, boat, buoy, or any sign of human life. We were still out there, deep in the pit of the Gulf, completely alone—with stinging rain, heavy winds, and huge waves—and we still had a long way to go.

Phillip and I bundled up and hunkered down at the helm and the boat performed beautifully that night. The waves were still four to six feet but she climbed them effortlessly and without complaint. It was as if the dinghy was the one bloody thorn in her heel. Now that we had pulled it out and rubbed the wound, she embraced us with gratitude and carried us through the storm. Phillip was a champion that night too. Aside from my relatively short, frequent shifts, he held the helm for about eight hours—without complaint—despite the steady heeling and rough waves. I had seen him impatient, uncomfortable, and irritated on occasion before, over far more insignificant things: when we had to wait for a table at a restaurant, for instance, when we were stuck in traffic, when someone had pissed him off at work. They were piddly things, mostly, and I was a bit shocked to see none of those emotions showing now, when we were wet, cold, achy, scared. I think Phillip truly saw this as his mission, his troop, and his obligation to get everyone—including the boat—home safely, without complaint. It must have been the Marine in him.

Once the sun came up the next morning, and we could finally see the horizon and the waves and assess our true state of affairs in

the daylight, my survival instincts sauntered to the background and my initial, adventurous tendencies returned. It's strange but every situation on the boat is amplified at night. Sails that dance and play during the day, flail and shriek at night. Waves that gently tousle you during the day, pitch and heave you violently at night. There's just something about being able to see the horizon and the open water around you for miles that makes everything feel safer, gentler, totally tolerable. *They said this crossing of the Gulf would be hard. Pish, tosh!* I whipped out the camera to begin, once again, documenting our tale. We had some dolphins spring up on the starboard side of the boat that morning, welcoming us in.

"They're our ambassadors," Phillip said. "They're bringing us in."

It certainly felt like they were. Finally we had sunlight, visibility, and now dolphins! We had it all. The wind was still cranking and the waves continued to toss us, but we had survived the night. We had lost the dinghy but we had saved the boat. We had made it! I felt like we were emerging at the mucky, muddy end of the pipes–stepping out, dirty and drenched in tunnel gunk, but alive, breathing in the clean air and squinting into the sunlight. The dolphins stayed with us for a while and I caught some footage of the friendly, finned ambassadors as we were making our way into the East Pass toward Apalachicola. http://youtu.be/wYOXuOrBMkk

We'd been out to sea for approximately thirty hours at that time–Phillip and I having spent about twenty-four of those in the cockpit or at the helm. After a good bit of nudging, a slightly-less ghastly Mitch finally rose to the light of day and joined us in the cockpit.

We made it into the Pass around noon and spotted land. The shelter from the shore gave us some much-needed relief from the wind. Once we made our way into the bay and turned toward Apalachicola–for the first time in over a day–we weren't beating into the wind, battling

broadside waves, and fighting for every nautical inch. We were now inside the bay with following winds, coasting through calmer, protected waters. But, most importantly, we were now on the *other* side of the Gulf. We had done it, crossed it, conquered it, put it behind us, and we all collectively breathed a sigh of relief having simply achieved it. Being in the bay–in the sunlight and comfort of visible shores–definitely put the crew and captain in good spirits.

We were eager to get to Apalachicola, get the boat secure and get ourselves to a hot shower. Trust me, while comfort and safety are the first things you begin to miss while on passage, cleanliness is a close second. After hours spent on-end at the helm–your hair and face all greasy, swaddled in the same sweaty clothes you were wearing the day and night before and unable to recall the last time you brushed your teeth–the only thing you want before sleep is a full-body hot water scouring.

We regained cell signal around noon and called the *Bottom Line* guys to check in. Finally, contact with our buddy! *Hey buddy! How you doing? How about that passage?*

"The Coast Guard," I heard Phillip say soon after he got them on the line, although I should say ask, rather, as his tone careened upward more in the form of a question than a statement. As it turned out, the *Bottom Line* crew had been trying to hail us on the radio throughout the night and–after hours of no contact–had reported to the Coast Guard that they had lost contact with us. *Reported? Us?* It kind of brought things home and reminded us how lucky we actually were to have made it across the Gulf in those conditions–particularly with the dangerous dinghy incident and a virgin crew. Looking back on it, the sacrifice of the dinghy had been a small price to pay. The *Bottom Line* guys were thankful to hear from us, finally, after a solid twenty-four hours of silence and said they would let the Coast Guard know we had made contact. *Made contact. Whew.* I imagined a red and white ship careening out through the Pass to go look for us. We were grateful, but a bit embarrassed as well, that we had caused them such worry.

After some tinkering with the radio that day, we learned we had not actually lost radio contact the night before. The handheld had certainly gone out–as a result of the repeated drenchings in the cockpit–but the main unit below worked fine *once* we disconnected the handheld. It made total sense, but it wasn't something that came immediately to mind when we were dicking around with the radio the night before. We found ourselves a bit embarrassed, but grateful again, that we did, in fact, have a functioning radio for the next leg of the trip. That's why they call it a "shakedown cruise" I imagine. You have to work out the kinks somehow.

The *Bottom Line* guys were about three hours ahead of us and just making their way into Apalachicola. Based on our heading and progress, we were set to pull into Apalachicola around 3:00 p.m., which was an immense relief. *Just a few more hours to go.* Our poor engine had been motoring now for almost twenty-four hours straight and she–more than any of us–was in dire need of a break. We motored along through the protected waters of the bay, enjoying the sights of land, other boats, a bridge–all soothing signs of civilization around us. Without the steady heeling of the boat port to starboard, Mitch finally began to perk and regain some color. It wasn't long before he started jabbering away as usual and eating everything in sight–granola bars, Bugles, fruit, chips, M&Ms, until it was time for lunch, and then he ate a sandwich, more chips, another granola bar, and more M&Ms.

He was a ravenous beast but, granted, he hadn't eaten anything since about the same time the day before. I'm sure he was starving.

We were all feeling pretty content and settled as we came upon the bridge to Apalachicola. We knew our mast height was fifty feet–a bit on the tall side for a sailboat–but the *Bottom Line* guys had told us the bridge was sixty-five feet, so we wouldn't have any trouble getting under. They had already made their way under it, but they also had a shorter mast than we did. The Captain, being the tedious sailor he is, would always check and double-check heights each time we come to a bridge. Phillip got the guy at the marina in Apalachicola (another Lou, Bob, Dick, Harry type) and asked about the bridge height. He told us he *thought* the bridge was fifty feet, could be sixty-five but he wasn't certain. *Thanks man, real helpful.* This troubled Phillip to no end. And for good reason. The time to learn your mast is too tall for a bridge is *not* right when you come up on it. Phillip pulled out the paper charts Jack had left on the boat to check the bridge height. Sure enough, the chart said it was fifty feet, which meant this boat was not going to be resting anytime soon and particularly not in Apalachicola. We weren't going to tango with that bridge. Phillip began looking for another marina where we could come in to dock for the night and we found we had passed the inlet for Carrabelle River about eight miles back.

And you might be thinking: *Eight miles? That's nothing. Whip around.* Yeah, I used to think that, too, until I realized our optimal speed in the boat is about four to five miles per hour. So eight miles back translated to another two-or-so hours backtracking in the bay–this time *against* the wind–and then another two to three hours

to get into the river and get docked. Likely another six hours total and it was 2:00 p.m. already. The news hit the crew like a swift kick to the gut. We were so tired already–tired of motoring, tired of being on that boat, tired of making this damn passage, and now, when we finally see an end in sight, we have to turn around and travel another six hours back the way we came? Mitch fumed. He was visibly pissed. I was disheartened but tried to keep a cheery front up for the Captain's sake. If the bridge was in fact only fifty feet tall, there was no other option. Although we would learn later that the bridge to Apalachicola was in fact a solid, sound sixty-five feet and that we could have made it under no problem–much like the dead-but-not-really radio during our Gulf Crossing–this little tidbit of useful knowledge came well after its immediate need. All I can say is you try to make the best decisions with the information you have available at the moment. So we turned around, left Apalachicola like a sad relative waving in the rearview mirror, and started heading back east toward Carrabelle.

We didn't reach the mouth of Carrabelle River until around 9:00 p.m. that night. It had been a very long day and an even longer night. Nerves were worn and it was clear we were trying not to snap at each other, but anything that had previously come across as an easy request or friendly suggestion was now taken as a personal attack. A simple request like, "Hey Mitch, can you hand me the flashlight?" somehow came across as "Hey Dumbass, I still can't see over here," and was responded to in kind–usually with an expletive and a snort. We were just exhausted. We'd been at sea for about thirty-six hours and the dinghy incident had really drained us. We were also hungry, which didn't help matters. All we wanted to do was dock, shower, eat, and rest–in that order.

Despite the sad excuses for markers, we were somehow able to find the entrance to the Carrabelle River on the GPS. Those pitiful half-sunk, half-lit buoys reminded me of a Charlie Brown Christmas tree. Thankfully though with a lot of squinting, pointing, and a few more expletives, we were able to make them out and make our way into the river. Phillip asked me to find us a marina on the river–whatever was closest that had fuel, water and pump-out–get directions in, and get us a transient slip for the night. It sounded like a tall order and, for me, it was. That's a lot to ask of a newbie sailor–a blonde one at that. *Directions? Are you kidding? Did he not recall the Clearwater incident and the hang a left after the "big" bridge?* But while Phillip was not as vocal as Mitch was about it, he was just as exhausted–if not far more so–and he had his hands full trying to pick his way into the unfamiliar entrance to the river. I Googled, punched in some numbers, and hoped for the best.

Another Dick-Lou-Harry-type character answered the phone with a "Yelloh." He was with The Moorings marina on Carrabelle River and, I swear to you, these were the *exact* directions he gave me:

"Just stay 'right of the river' till you get around the bend, then you'll see our fuel sign." I've grown to learn this is a typical instruction from your average, everyday dockmaster. Not knowing at all what to expect in the river or where he was located, I felt like he'd given me zip. I asked Dick-Lou-Harry several times for clarification—not wanting us to repeat the same go-round-in-circles procedure we'd had to do when coming into Clearwater because the directions I got then were so blasé as well—but that's all the dockmaster would give me.

"Just stay right of the river and you won't have any problem." *Right of the river.* I have to admit I was a bit confused. I was sure he meant stay on the right *side* of the river. Surely that's what "right *of*" meant. But I'd never quite heard it put *that way.* And, mind you, this inquisition was coming from one with a good bit of country directional terms—up yonder, down yonder, past the ditch, up a ways, etc. But I guess I had not yet been introduced to *nautical* country and I was clearly struggling. I came up to the cockpit and relayed the directions to Phillip, watching his face closely for what I was sure was going to be disapproval. His shoulders dropped and he looked me dead-on and asked, "Right of the river?" He had the same reaction as I did. What *exactly* did that mean? Well we were about to learn.

We started into the river—trying to stay on the right side as much as possible—but Carrabelle River is about one hundred yards across in some places, pretty narrow for a sailboat. The left bank was marshy and overgrown and the right bank was littered with docks and piers and homemade sea walls. There were also plenty of boats docked up on the right side, jutting out and forcing us more toward the "middle" of the river than the "right." It was also hard to see in the river at night. There were just a few little pier lights and street lights casting a light glow on the water. We found a great spotlight on the boat only to find the DC inlet it plugged into wasn't working—another shakedown fiasco. So, we relied solely on the squint-and-point method and kept checking the depth gauge every few seconds. Mitch saw some other sailboats anchored up ahead on the left side of the river, which gave us some comfort, but apparently too much. Mitch was pointing and we were all looking ahead, trying to make them out, when the boat came to an immediate, gut-halting stop. We all lurched forward as a thick, muddy sound erupted from the river. *We had run aground.*

FIFTEEN

Did He Say Curly Fries?

"The Captain always," and he would pause for effect, "goes down," another pause, "with the ship." It required a precise amount of pauses, an exact degree of dramatic flair, and—a must—the waving of his cowboy hat above his head during the first part and then the planting of it respectfully on his chest like he's pledging allegiance during the last. At least that's the way my dad tells it. It's another one of those Runt stories that I love. Runt was one of dad's best friends in high school and—weighing approximately 120 pounds soaking wet and standing at a towering five foot, five inches in heeled boots—he was quite deserving of the name. Runt was the boys' guinea pig, their occasional sacrificial lamb, and their go-to test dummy for all of the crazy, stupid cowboy things the guys felt they needed need to do. Stories about Runt often involve waving hats and, for some reason, the delicate placing of the hat on the chest in humble salute. I guess Runt used to do that a lot because dad often mimics it when he tells a good Runt tale.

There are so many, like the time the boys bent a young pine over and launched Runt out of the top of it way out into Smith Lake. He was

fully clothed, mind you, and, as always, sailing through the air straight as a pin with his cowboy hat pressed against his chest until he smashed into the water about a quarter mile out. "A quarter mile, at least!" my dad would say. "We didn't know if he was gonna be able to swim it back." Then there was the time they dared Runt one night, when he was stumbling-down drunk (which is a specific kind of drunk), to try and ride Old Man Hendrick's prize-winning hog. Legend has it the hog bit Runt while he was trying to tie a bucking belt on him and Runt punched him square in the face. Can you imagine? Punching a hog in the face? I can't even remember how the actual hog ride went down. I forgot everything after the punch. But, of all the wild Runt rumors, legends, and tales, "The Captain Story" would forever remain my favorite.

Apparently my dad, Runt, and their two other high school cowboy compadres–Big Mike and Billy Jack–decided it a fine idea one night to sneak off in my dad's sister, De's, truck. The boys were somewhere around sixteen at the time–not quite driving age yet or at least not quite in possession of their own truck if they were. So, they would often bum rides–truckpool I guess you would call it when it's not done in a car–and, as the occasion called for it, sneak out in Aunt De's old '57 Chevy–all four of them squished up together in the bench seat like a clown car. Back then De parked her truck on the uphill drive at Big Mom's and if the boys were planning to sneak it out that night, they would put Runt behind the wheel to steer and brake, put the truck in neutral, and push it on down the driveway to the county road before cranking it so they wouldn't wake anyone at the house. While my dad kind of skirts around the details, you know Big Mike snuck a fifth of whiskey from his granddad's barn that evening and, by the end of it, it was one of them stumbling-down nights. Runt was driving and they were all laughing and joking and spitting in cans on the way home when they came up on a long stretch of road submerged in water. It had rained hard that day in Cullman and the drainage on the county roads was never good. The hooting and cussing whimpered out as Runt slowed the truck and they all eyed the road ahead, none of them having ever seen it that flooded. Before they could think twice about it though, Runt slammed on the gas and started barreling toward the road-pond, shouting "Hold on boys!" as he blazed into the water, kicking up a wake five feet on either side of the truck. It wasn't long before the wheels were spinning in water, gripping nothing, and the truck lurched forward to a watery halt and started to sink.

Dad says water started to rush into the floorboard of the truck the minute he opened the door. The boys tried to get out and push the truck backward but it had too much forward momentum and was sinking fast. The water on the road was far deeper than they had thought and soon they were up to their waists in it, wading back to high ground. As they looked back for Runt, they saw him scrambling out of the driver's side window, trying to crawl up on top of the cab of the truck, his spurs catching and hanging on the seatbelt. He finally made his way topside, stood clumsily on the cab of the truck, and turned to face the boys standing wet and dripping on the side of the road. Runt straightened his back, squared his shoulders, and with feigned solemnity, belted into the night.

"The Captain," hat held high in the air. "Always," hat wave one way. "Goes down," hat wave the other. "With the ship," as he placed it respectfully on his chest and stood stoically looking out above the boys' heads, to some invisible flag flying in the distance. The truck gurgled down some but stopped anticlimactically soon after his speech, the water coming only about halfway up the engine, never even nearing Runt's boots on top of the cab. Dad says Runt stood there a bit longer, hat-to-chest, holding his stoic pose, until they all started snickering and doubling over with laughter. The crazy part is, De never found out. With some creative use of a rope, a tractor, and a nearby tree, they were able to pull the truck out of the water, let her dry out until sunrise, and—much to their surprise—she cranked and gurgled home. The wet cab was chalked up to rain leaking through an inadvertently-cracked window and no one was ever the wiser. While John couldn't manage to hide his swindle of a fifth of rum from Big Mom, dad was able to somehow hide his theft of an entire truck? Although there was no ship and no real danger, Runt's heroic offer to accompany the truck to the depths of the road-pond were never forgotten.

I couldn't help but think of that gurgling, sinking truck as we now found ourselves lurching into the thick mud of the Carrabelle River, slowly listing to port as the boat dug in, thinking there was a good chance we too might sink. After having spent thirty-six hours at sea–crossing the entire Gulf of Mexico–it sickened me to think the boat might meet its ultimate demise here in the damn river, not one hundred feet from shore. And here was the Captain, Phillip, standing behind the wheel, ready as Runt to go down with the ship. I couldn't believe it.

But thankfully it seems if you're going to run aground, the best place to do it is in thick, soft river mud. Phillip threw her in reverse and she lurched out, with a loud, muddy smack. We all let out a monstrous sigh of relief and started looking around, apparently with new clarity, because it wasn't until *then* that we noticed right in front of our faces a string of red day markers–no lights on them, of course, that would be too much to ask–but they formed a defined line well beyond the middle of the river, showing us how far out the shoal came. *Thanks anyway crappy markers. We found it with the bottom of our boat!* The markers left only a narrow channel between the shoal and the docks and piers on the right bank that was deep enough to travel. It was clear Dick-Lou-Harry really meant *right* of the freaking river. Phillip rolled his eyes and shook his head but kept on.

We made it to the marina and docked with ease. No crazy pole-lassoing this time and no corn-fed hosses holding us off the dock. The river was protected from winds and we were a bit more experienced at bringing her in. We got her tied up and buttoned down and hit the showers. Having traveled many-a-mile from New Mexico to Alabama and back with my dad in his old Peterbilt, I have to say the showers at this marina reminded me of somewhat dressed-up truck-stop showers. Although some stalls had flimsy, torn curtains, most had none at all, so they were pretty much like gym-class community showers, but someone coming in while I was showering was the least of my worries. After everything I'd been through in the last thirty-six hours, I could care less if anyone wanted to get a free sneak peek at my battered, beaten body. And, if anyone tried to get a little too friendly in the shower, I was sure I could handle them. I'd whip out my Crocodile Dundee knife and tell them I'd do to them what I'd done to my pal Dinghy in the middle of the Gulf. Nothing was going to ruin my shower. Truth is though we were all so exhausted and smelly and dirty and salty, any rusty spigot that dribbled tepid little droplets of water on us would have easily been deemed the best shower we'd ever had. It's amazing how uncomfortable conditions can make you truly appreciate the smallest amenities of your everyday life. The luke-warm drizzle-shower in the truck-stop community bathroom that night felt like a lavish pampering at a resort spa.

The minute I started scrubbing and inspecting my battered body, Barbara's words came tumbling back into my mind. "You'll look like you've been in a motor vehicle accident," she had said. And boy did I. Every bony prominence–the outside of my hips, both elbows, those two little points above your buttocks, even my ass–had deep, purple bruises on them. Not to mention the multiple dings, bumps, and scrapes along my shins, knees, and hands. All of that heeling–left to right, left to right–makes you use parts of your body you had never thought to use before to brace yourself, bruising be damned. The boat heels sharp to starboard and you've got a flashlight in one hand and the Gorton's hat in the other. What do you do? Wedge your hip into the nav station and a knee against the stairs until it passes. Then the boat heels just as sharply back to port and you're halfway up the stairs–yes, still with the flashlight and the Gorton's Hat. I mean, you are carrying them for a reason, I hope. What do you do? Wedge a shin into a stair and push your butt against the countertop till it passes. You just do it without thinking about it. Walking around on the boat while it's heeling left and right like that starts to look like a Foxtrot after a while. It's heel-wedge-hold for three beats, three quick steps forward, then another heel-wedge-hold for three more beats, then two more quick steps. Can you just hear the music now? It's like an elegant ballroom dance but without the elegance. I was shocked at how many bruises I had developed without really being aware of it. My limbs, hips, and arms were littered with purple, green, and blue blobs. Barb was right. I looked like I'd been T-boned by a damn Cadillac. But, for whatever reason my mind flashed back to that foul bath, my fizzling skin and the look on Big Mom's face as she swished hydrogen peroxide and spat. *You're alive ain't ya?* her voice wafted into my stall.

"You're damn right I am!" I told myself, in that grimy little tiled shower stall–sudsing up my hair with a big fat smile on my face. *You're damn right I am.*

I was second back to the boat after our showers. Every muscle and joint ached as I climbed on-board to find Mitch stretched out on the starboard settee. I mean laid out the full length–arms behind his head, ankles crossed–totally kicked back and he asks me, "So … are you going to make that sausage tonight for dinner?" I know I heard a record-scratch somewhere. Time stopped–at least for a second. I wish I could have seen my face when he asked me that. Because if he was thinking it was my job, after *that* passage, to cook anyone anything for dinner, I was thinking I was going to slap him–right across the face, or upside the head, I couldn't quite decide. That would at least make up for the many slaps he'd laid on me when we were grabbing lines, pulling sheets, and wrestling sails. Calling *me* "Girlie?" Mr. Non-Drowsy Dramamine who slept through about twelve hours of our harrowing ordeal. *Cook him some sausage.* I was going to kill him. And I might have, had Phillip not stepped down into the cabin at that very moment.

I turned my back to Mitch, looked at Phillip and told him I was going to go check the dock lines while *someone* got some sausage started for Mitch for dinner because Mitch was hungry. Phillip looked at me a little funny when I told him that–much like I had when Mitch told me–but I said nothing. I just gave Phillip a you-figure-it-out expression as I passed him on the way up the stairs. I don't know what conversation ensued while I went topside to emit some hot fumes but when I came back down Mitch was setting the table and pouring me a glass of wine. We all made dinner together and never mentioned it. There wasn't any need. We were all tired, we were all hungry, and I'm sure it was just his caveman instinct kicking in. "I am man. Feed me." I could forgive him of that.

We inhaled our food, eyelids drooping and heads bobbing, and went straight to bed. I don't think I've slept that hard since my last college bender. Okay, we all know my last bender was well after college but the college ones were far more epic. We woke up a little disoriented and groggy the next morning—each of us blinking and looking at each other suspiciously, wondering where exactly we were and why we felt like we'd been run over by a Mac truck. We rallied quickly though, cracked some jokes about community showers and sausage, and started readying the boat for the last leg of the passage. We were about a day and a half behind schedule but we had crossed the Gulf. That was the hard part we thought. It was supposed to be easy after this. Our plan was to make our way back out the East Pass, cruise up along the coast to Panama City for a quick stop at the marina there, overnight if necessary, before making the last leg of the trip from Panama City to Pensacola Pass late the following evening.

We all moved with a little more spring in our step as we untied the lines and pitched them on to the boat. Even the engine seemed to have a fresh little hum about her when she cranked that morning and puttered us over to the fuel dock. It seemed she had got a much-needed, full-night's rest as well. We all worked systematically as we fueled up, pumped out, and filled the water tanks. It was surprising—after just a few short days together on the boat–how well we were functioning as a crew. Granted they had been some very trying days but it was nice to see us working in such synchronized harmony. As Mitch pulled the hose to the boat to fill the water tanks, I came up with the key to open the little screw-down lid and help him. Phillip took the key from me when we finished to open the fuel lid and fill the diesel. Phillip also topped off the oil and checked the coolant to make sure our baby was ready to carry us home in case we faced another harrowing thirty hours motoring in the Gulf. Everything looked right as rain, so we waved to the friendly folk at the fuel dock and headed back out the Carrabelle River–this time to the extreme *left* to avoid that thick muddy shoal we'd left our mark in the night before. It was around 7:00 a.m., the sun was just coming up behind the houses on the left bank of the river, and we were breathing in the morning, eager to get back out and under way.

I even joked with Mitch on my way down below to start the coffee and make breakfast. "I'll bet you could go for some sausage this morning, huh Mitch?" I asked him with a smile as I headed down the companionway stairs. But just as I started to fill the kettle, a deafening blare filled the galley. It was the sound the engine makes when you turn the key just before starting it, and it was a somewhat familiar sound–in that I had heard it often during the trip–but it was usually one sound in a series of several other familiar sounds that ended with the cranking of the engine. Click, beep, rumble, crank. This was just the beep. No rumble. No crank. Just a shrill, lonesome, ear-piercing beep was all I heard. Then it dawned on me that the engine wasn't running. Yes, it took a moment for the revelation to blossom. But, that's why the beep seemed so loud and persistent. The engine had stopped, leaving only the beep. Footsteps thundered overhead on the deck as I heard Phillip shout, "Mitch, go get the … " something or-'nother to Mitch who I assumed was running toward the bow of the boat. I couldn't make out what Phillip had said but the tone in his voice was urgent. I scrambled up the stairs to the cockpit and saw Phillip looking frantically about, his hands on the key and ignition.

"Did you try to re-crank it?" Mitch shouted back to him. Phillip looked at me and rolled his eyes. It was a legitimate question but I mean, really? *Nope, I'm just sitting back here watching the wind blow.* I could tell by now that we were having engine trouble but I have to admit, as a sailing newbie that still didn't worry me immediately. *Jeepers Cap'n. The engine won't crank? Are we in a pickle?* That is seriously what ran through my mind. *Is this a big deal?*

Then I looked out and the gravity of our dire situation set in. We were floating helplessly along the river–the narrow, shallow river–the one with the muddy shoal that had almost sunk us the night before, the one with expensive boats lined up at docks on either side of us. And without the engine, we had no way to stop ourselves from crashing into any one of those options–the bank, the bottom, the half-a-million-dollar Catamaran that we were drifting effortlessly toward. It then dawned on me why Mitch had run up to the bow. He was trying to drop the anchor to stop us. Phillip started throwing dock lines and buckets out of the lazarette on the port side.

"We need the other anchor," he said tersely, which was my

cue to help him dig it out. We both started grabbing and throwing lines, jamming our hands into the lazarette as fast as we could to get everything out because of course–*of course!*–the anchor was on the very bottom. I tore a huge chunk out of my knuckle in the process that I only discovered later by following the blood trail back to the lazarette. We finally got the secondary, danforth anchor out and chunked it overboard–feeding out line frantically, hoping she would catch. We looked up to see where we were drifting and the owner of the half-a-million-dollar Catamaran–who had previously been gingerly polishing his boat on this fine morning, wiping away any small spots and specks–was now watching a thirty-five-foot, fifteen thousand pound, give-or-take sailboat head straight for it. I gripped the line to the anchor and watched as the Catamaran guy stood up and stretched his neck tall like a crane–his hose now hanging aimlessly, splashing water loudly on his deck–and his eyes opening wide as we inched closer.

We all stood helpless, watching our boat make its way closer and closer to the Catamaran. I closed my eyes and gritted my teeth–the only thing I knew to do at the moment–while my mind conjured horrific images of boat crashes. Just as I was bracing for the worst, I felt a slight tug on the anchor line. It had caught. *Finally.* I gripped hard and shouted to Phillip. We didn't want to yank it up so he said it was best to let some line out and let it dig in a bit. A dicey proposition when your boat is headed straight for one three times the price but it wouldn't help anything if the anchor slipped. I let some more line inch through my hands as the boat slowed. *Finally.* We eased up to the Catamaran with just enough room for the guy to push us off of his glistening gem. We handed him a line and he helped us walk our boat over to an empty spot at the dock next to him and tie up. The relief of having the boat stopped and secure made us forget momentarily about the engine. *Engine? What engine?* At least, for now, she was tied up and not going anywhere.

The Catamaran guy was a big help though and quite understanding. Turns out he also had a boat that was broke down on the other side of the river. It seems engine problems are common in the boating community. We joked that there must be something in the water but that was actually a legitimate concern. We checked the fuel pump to see if it was clogged and preventing fuel intake, or wasn't separating the water from the fuel, but it seemed fine. We checked the impeller–where the boat pulls in sea water as a coolant for the engine–to make sure it wasn't clogged, which could have caused the engine to overheat. But no dice there either. We simply had no answers. We had checked and filled the oil that morning, checked the coolant, gassed up, and she had cranked fine. She was *running* fine, up until the moment she wasn't. We felt like the guys on *King of the Hill*, just standing around scratching, drinking, and wiggling a wire here and there but with no real progress–a sort of lawn mower focus group if you will.

Phillip tried to crank her a couple more times but she wouldn't even turn over. It was almost like she had a dead battery but we knew that wasn't the case because the house batteries were full and running fine. We were at a loss. Phillip had me get on the phone and try to find a mechanic that could come out and take a look at the engine.

The bad news was most of them were located in Apalachicola–a good 30 minutes away–without the resources or time to make a special emergency trip to the Carrabelle River to check us out. Thankfully after a handful of calls and some groveling and pleading, we were lucky enough to find a willing victim. He worked out of a marina just around the bend in the river from where we had docked, which he had been operating out of for over twenty years. His family even owned a little bar and grille on the Carrabelle River–Fathom's. In those parts, if you needed a good diesel engine guy, *he* was your man. Eric. Our savior.

Eric had a big job on a barge to get to that day but he told us he'd stop by on his way out to see if our problem could be fixed quickly and if he could, perhaps, get us back on our way that day. Eric arrived within the hour and he was super sharp. He immediately began tinkering and turning bolts, troubleshooting and crossing items off of his differential diagnosis. We were glad to see him roll up his sleeves and go to work so quickly. Our boat seemed to whisper a small "thank you" to us. But Eric, unfortunately, kept coming up empty-handed. We continued our super-helpful practice of standing there, watching, wire-wiggling, and scratching but apparently it wasn't enough. Eric came up greasy, sweaty, and shaking his head in defeat. He was going to have to take the engine apart to figure it out but he had to get out to the barge that was waiting on him. Eric said he would send his guys back out in a couple of hours to get to work on our boat.

We waved Eric off as we sat on the dock, next to our broke-down boat, to figure out what to do. We were approaching high noon–a very hot high noon–and we were tired and drained and exceedingly weary from the passage. Noon meant one thing for Mitch and he scampered off to go check out the local food situation, while Phillip and I sat on the dock baking in the heat. We were frustrated with the situation, waiting for the engine boys to come back, both of us thinking of any place we'd rather be than stranded there on a hot dock with a broke-down boat. But we had a tough decision to make. It was already noon, on the day we *thought* we would have made it back to Pensacola and we still had another forty-eight hour passage ahead of us. That was assuming the engine could be fixed on the spot and assuming no other malfunctions along the way—all very big assumptions. The possibility of even making it back to Pensacola by the end of the week looked grim.

If work had been weighing on us two days prior back in Clearwater, it was pressing down on us like a hot iron now. We were a four-hour drive from home but, by boat, a three-day passage, at best, after the repairs. Phillip and I talked it through and decided we had to call it. We were going to have to leave the boat at the marina in Carrabelle and make the drive home by car. We were truly disheartened. Phillip and I wanted to make this passage, to bring our boat back to its new homeport, make the dream a reality. But we just didn't have the time to spare, especially with the status of the engine currently a complete unknown. It could be hours, days—weeks even—before the boat was fully functional again. We hated the thought of leaving her there—alone, miles away from home, without any answers—and we hated the thought of coming back to Pensacola in some crappy rental car, when we were supposed to sail in on crystal green waters, in our shiny new boat. But we knew we had to do it. Phillip and I sat somberly on the dock, one apologetic hand on the boat as Mitch bounded up from the dilapidated dock restaurant behind us like a loopy Tigger.

"The sign says they open in half an hour. Do you think they'll have curly fries?" he asked. "I could really go for some curly fries."

For the second time in two days I found myself contemplating his murder, except there would be no slapping this time. This time it involved choking him. With curly fries.

SIXTEEN

A Dasani Bottle and Some Duct Tape

"Hang on a sec," he said as he rushed out from behind the counter. "I need to bring this Cessna in."

I watched him as he grabbed a headset and a pair of those little airplane-guiding Jedi light sticks and ran out the door. Not only did the Apalachicola airport double as the only car rental agency in town, it was a travel agency, insurance office, and coin-operated laundromat. Apparently they like to squeeze a lot of things into one in the Big Bend. He was quick and efficient though and he had me outfitted in one of their hot little crossover SUVs in no time. The drive from Carrabelle to Pensacola was long and lackluster. We were leaving the boat behind–with no answers, no timeline, no clue as to what was even wrong, how long it was going to take to get her fixed, or worse, how much it was going to cost.

It was several days before we got a call from Eric, the mechanic in Carrabelle, with some good news and some bad. He had taken the engine apart and it didn't seem the problem was with the engine. He initially had thought that water on the heads was preventing the engine from turning but he had taken it apart and found no water. He then found what he thought could be metal shavings in the oil filter which he told us was a particularly bad sign. That meant something in the engine had likely failed and locked up but he examined the entire engine, top to bottom, and found nothing. That left the transmission, which Eric planned to take apart and have a look at in the next few days.

Phillip and I were a bit relieved that it wasn't the engine. Replacing those puppies can be very expensive, with the cost of a new engine running in the ten-K range. Of course that's just the cost of the engine. That doesn't include the labor to put it in and actually install it, which is another couple grand–not a small chunk of change and not a price anyone is happy to pay, particularly right after we had just shelled out some serious change to *buy* the dang boat in the first place. So the fact that it wasn't the transmission did, technically, qualify as good news. However, we were not pleased to hear about the metal shavings and suspected catastrophic failure of some surely-useful metal part. It didn't take long for Mechan-Eric to figure out what it was and I have to say it is *kind of* important. It was the transmission–the thing that actually shifts into gear and, you know, propels the boat forward or backward. *Yeah, that's pretty useful.*

Turns out we had run the transmission completely out of fluid during the epic thirty-six-hour crossing, causing it to overheat and lock-up. While we certainly appreciated the news, it was not well received by our lawn mower focus group. We were really shocked by it. Like a car, the transmission fluid is not something you regularly check on a boat—at least not as much as the oil or the coolant. When we chatted with our fellow boat friends about it, they all agreed the transmission fluid is not something they check regularly on their boats and some—names omitted to protect the guilty—even admitted they hadn't checked theirs in years, but they certainly would now! We'd also had a survey done on the boat just one month prior to our Gulf crossing and assumed all of the fluids had been checked then. "Surely Kip checked that," we said to ourselves. *And surely he would have let us know if it was low,* I thought. *Surely.*

We had also had no problems with the transmission during the passage—no issues shifting gears, no sign at all that the transmission was struggling. Like I said the boat ran, shifted and chugged along perfectly up until the moment it didn't run at all. It was incredibly irritating to find the reason we had to call the trip and leave the boat docked up at a diesel mechanic's marina in Carrabelle was a simple lack of transmission fluid. Why? Because: a) transmission fluid is super cheap—like a buck forty-nine a jug or something, and b) we'd *had* some on the boat at the time. We just hadn't poured it in. What's worse (and this is Mitch's ultimate redemption) when Phillip was checking the fluids that fateful morning in Carrabelle—the oil, the coolant, the gas, etc.—he asked Mitch to hand him the engine oil so he could top it off and Mitch had inadvertently handed him the transmission fluid instead.

OH THE IRONY!

Yes, irony—the opposite of wrinkly—as in, "Gee Ted, how did you get your shirt so starched and irony?" And of course it was Mitch—of all people–the man whom I'd contemplated suffocating with curly fries who had tried to save our asses that day but we'd turned him down. *Transmission fluid? Please, that's crazy talk! She just needs oil boss.* It was just as Alanis had predicted–like "ray-eey-ain" on our wedding day. When we looked back on it, Phillip and I couldn't believe Mitch had almost saved us. Almost. But more so, we couldn't believe we had run the thing slap out of fluid. *Really?* Thirty-eight cents-worth of that pink nectar dumped in there and it would have saved us? We would have pulled right out of the Carrabelle River and sailed her home weeks ago? Now we were looking at putting a new transmission on a boat we *just* bought? But it could have been worse I guess. At least that's what we told ourselves. It could have blown the entire engine. This was just the transmission and we learned a very valuable lesson: always, *always*, check all–and I do mean all–of the fluids before you crank the engine. We do it now–every fluid, before every crank–especially the transmission fluid.

Of course that is now. This was then. *Then* we were looking at shelling out another $2,500 for a new transmission–not to mention the labor to have it put in–because we hadn't checked the dang fluid. *Bullocks!* It was no use griping about it though. I'll bet those same kids that don't get breakfast don't have boats either, am I right? It was only the transmission, so we sucked it up and gave Eric the okay to replace it. He soon found a used transmission on Craigslist that was just right. *A big thanks to Craig and his handy dandy list!* Some sailboat guru down in Jacksonville had a brand new transmission he had bought a year ago for a project boat that he never got around to. *A boat project you never got around to? Impossible!* But, his loss was our gain. We doled out the dough and the transmission was ours. Eric would receive it in a week's time and have it installed and have our engine up and running again in another.

In the meantime Phillip and I couldn't just leave our boat sitting there all alone in a strange place—weird barnacles growing on her, strange fish nipping at her, and no one there to wipe her deck and tell her how "purdy" she is. *Uh-huh. Not our boat!* So we headed down to the ol' Apalach area several times to pay her a visit and give her a little TLC while she sat wounded and torn apart at the marina. In all our boat spent about six weeks at the Carrabelle marina having the transmission replaced and we spent that time planning the last leg of the passage. This time Phillip and I were going to do it alone—just he and I, the Captain and his country counterpart. It seemed I'd earned some nautical stripes during our first passage and Phillip thought we were ready to make some overnight passages together—just the two of us. I was tickled hot pink. It felt like getting picked first in P.E. "Me? You mean *me*?" you say, with a look back over either shoulder and a stiff point to your chest. We were really going to do this. Phillip and I. Cruise the coast in our sailboat. This was it!

"Ju-ust the two of us. We can make it if we try-yy." I sang it all the time while we were planning and plotting our passage, provisioning and packing our gear. We were going to drive down to Carrabelle on a Friday, settle up with Mechan-Eric and make sure the boat was in working order, and then head back out bright and early on Saturday morning through the East Pass to make the quick, twenty-four-hour jaunt along the coast up to Panama City. We would stop there and rest for a night at the marina and then head back offshore to make the last leg of the trip–another twenty-two hours or so from Panama City up to Pensacola Pass–to bring our boat to her new home in Pensacola where she belonged. *Finally!*

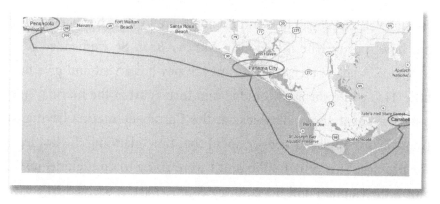

We vowed this time to wait for a good weather window and to build in an extra two-to-three-day cushion just in case, well, in case anything that *could* possibly go wrong *did* go wrong and we would need some extra time to get it repaired, fixed, or otherwise handled in order to get back on course. We had definitely learned from our last trip that a tight window for travel was a dangerous proposition. We were not going to tango with *time* this go-round. If the conditions weren't right, we would wait.

We enlisted our trusty sail groupies again–Phillip's folks–to haul us and our gear, once again, down the coast to Carrabelle to drop us off for the passage. They must be gluttons for punishment because they agreed wholeheartedly, and we enjoyed a great afternoon poking

around the sleepy downtown of Apalachicola before making our way on further to Carrabelle. At the marina Mechan-Eric walked us through everything he had done and cranked the engine for us. It was the first time we had heard her turn over in six weeks. She grumbled and sputtered and started roaring! I don't think I've ever heard a more glorious sound. She was *running*. Our engine was running! Eric showed us the transmission, which he had painted a bright, cherry red to match the signature Westerbeke color of the engine, and shifted her through the gears—drive, neutral and reverse—so we could see the transmission at work. Everything looked great. Everything shifted perfectly. We gave it the old Roger Ebert and we were ready to go! I swear I could feel her little stern wagging as we slept in the v-berth that night–like a sad-eyed puppy at the pound that had finally been picked. We were going to scoop her up and take her home with us. First thing in the morning!

Now I would love to say we woke that morning with a stretch and yawn and cute bunny smack but we didn't. We woke to the sound of gerbils–angry, evil, little turkey-gobbling gerbils–or at least that's what I would imagine it would sound like, if four of them were stuffed in a sock together, all wrestling and rabid. They were birds, actually–angry birds–and while they did rob us that morning of a slow, slumbering rouse, we didn't really care. We were ready to get that boat a-going! We checked the fluids–gas, oil, coolant and transmission. *Of course!* Like I said we will never again, until our little sailing hearts stop beating, *not* check the transmission fluid before we crank the engine. Whether it's been a half hour or four days, we want to see that dipstick coated in sweet, pink nectar before we'll even think about turning the engine over. With the fluids properly checked, we readied the sails, tossed the lines, and headed out into the Carabelle River. We puttered along–knowing full well *this* time which side of the river to stay on–made it out into the Gulf right at sunrise and it was like she rose just for us. It can certainly feel that way sometimes when you're sailing. Because no one else is out there to see it. It's just you, your boat, and an endless horizon, like the world is spinning just for you.

And, this time it was just us–Phillip and I–off on our first couple's cruise. We brewed up a hot batch of hazelnut coffee, nestled in the cockpit, and watched every minute of the sunrise. While Mitch had

certainly been an asset on the first trip, it was great this time to embrace the serenity and put our newly-formed team-sailing skills to the test. We were taking her back out again in blue waters and finally sailing her home—just the two of us.

There wasn't much wind so we were motoring most of the morning but I could have spent all day in that cockpit, sipping coffee, holding the helm, curled up with a book or my laptop, just watching the water float by. I was perfectly content. Nothing crossed my mind other than the soft lapping of the water on the hull and the sweet scent of the saltwater in the air. But that's why I'm only the first mate and Phillip is the Captain. Thankfully he had the wherewithal to think to check on the engine. I mean she had been sitting for a month, she just had a new transmission put in, and we had been running her now for about an hour and a half. *Yep, it might be a good idea to check on her.* That's why Phillip's the brains. I'm the brawn.

Phillip gave me the helm and went down below to see how things were looking under the "hood," which in our boat is akin to looking under the sink. In order to access the engine on the Niagara, we pull back a hinged "L-shaped" piece that houses the sink and utensil drawers and set it back against the table in the salon to provide access to the engine.

As I held the wheel I could hear Phillip down below pull the sink back, set it against the table, and click on a flashlight to take a look at the engine. It reminded me of that first night we spent on the boat in Clearwater where I had first begun to really see the boat as a true home–with all of the incumbent sounds, smells, nooks and crannies. It surprised me now how familiar I already was with the boat in that, from the cockpit, I could tell what Phillip was doing down below by sound alone. I saw his beam moving in and around the engine and I could hear him wiggling some things and tinkering around. I wouldn't have thought much of it had his silence not continued for just a little too long. Minutes passed and he didn't pop his head up and give me a thumbs up, or say "Everything looks great," or "Good to go," or anything like that. He was just quiet–*too* quiet. I wanted to ask him how everything was going, but I knew he'd tell me when it was time and a part of me didn't want to know. Good news blurts out easy. Bad news takes longer to formulate. I was perfectly content to sit up there at the wheel, whistling tunes to myself, pretending we didn't even have an engine, or fluids, or any of that. *Engine? What engine? I'm cruising along just fine up here. Doop-de-doo.*

But Phillip finally raised his head in the companionway and gave me the exact look I was fearing. Something was wrong. He told me to put on the autopilot and summoned me down. I came down the stairs and he handed me the flashlight without saying a word, which worried me even more. Although, after the initial leg of The Crossing, I was certainly far *more* familiar with the engine than I had been before, I was still no diesel mechanic. If the problem was obvious enough for me to *see* with my naked eye, it was probably bad. And it was. Underneath the engine and slithering on down to the bilge was a bright, pink trail of fluid.

Phillip and I were hoping it was just some of that famous Westerbeke Red paint Mechan-Eric had sprayed on the transmission to make it match the rest of the engine. *No, big deal. Just some paint. Surely that's it.* But, as it always seems, life can never be that simple. Having run the old transmission slap out of fluid the last time, we were all too familiar with that pink viscous liquid to be pretty darn sure what was trickling out of our engine was more likely transmission fluid than paint. Phillip then showed me what he had found during his wiggling and tinkering: a transmission fluid leak.

Little red drops kept forming—one after the other under the shifter arm of the transmission—and falling to a grey grave below in the bilge. There was no denying it. Our brand new, bright red, *painfully* expensive transmission was leaking. I felt like I could have cried too—a little red trail of tears behind it right down to the bilge.

  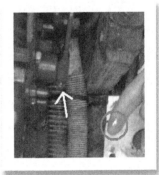

Oh the irony again! During our last passage the transmission was perfectly sealed—no leaks to be had—and we had run her completely out of fluid unwittingly. Now we were keenly aware of the level of fluid in the transmission, hypersensitive to its lubrication needs, and now the precious pink fluid was dripping out non-stop, constantly sacrificing itself to the bilge below? *Stop! Wait! Come back!* It was kind of funny. *Kind of.* But we were two hours from Carrabelle, twelve hours from our next stop, with little wind and only a half quart of transmission fluid to go on. The same half-quart, actually, that Mitch had tried to hand us that fateful morning in Carrabelle. I'll bet his greasy fingerprints were still on it and I could just see him now: leaned back, fingers steepled, his body racked with the bellowing "Muuu-ha-haaa" laugh of an evil villain. *Damn you Mitch!* I screamed it inside but I knew it was futile, and wrong. Mitch had nothing to do with this. Perhaps this was no one's fault, but we should have picked up more fluid before we left Carrabelle in case, well, in case of anything–another shakedown lesson learned.

We didn't have time to sit and mourn our sad state of affairs though. Every drop of fluid that splashed to the bilge put us one drop further from home and we had a long way to go. We were only two hours into an approximately forty-eight-hour trip. We had very little wind that morning. It might have been blowing three miles per hour, if it was blowing at all. And it was blowing out of the southwest–right on our nose–so it certainly wasn't working with us. We weren't going to get anywhere sailing. The one good thing about being only two hours out was that we still had cell reception. We called Mechan-Eric to see if he had any brilliant ideas. Unfortunately he didn't answer his phone and we had to leave a message, advising him of the transmission drip coming out of our shifter arm. You can just imagine the agony of the next few minutes while we watched little tiny pink drops fall to an untimely death in the bilge–one after the other–while I constantly checked my phone.

Slide to unlock. Click. No messages.

Tick, tock.

Slide to unlock. Click. No messages.

Drip, drop.

Then–*finally!*–my phone shimmied and vibrated on the nav station, like a happy little bee. Such a glorious sound. I clawed and clicked that thing open faster than I ever have before. It was Eric calling back with what he said he thought was "good news." Recall the guy we bought the new transmission from had bought it brand new for his own project boat that he–as many men often do–couldn't seem to find the time for. So the transmission sat on a shelf for over a year before it made its way to our engine. Eric said he had seen this happen before. When a new engine component sits for a while the little rubber gaskets inside dry-rot and have to be replaced. Eric was sure that was it–just a simple little ninety-six-cent gasket. An easy fix.

"Just keep pouring more fluid in and you can replace the gasket when you get home," he said. "Good news, right?"

Wrong Eric. Very wrong. We didn't have that much "more" to pour in. Mitch's evil villain laugh rang out in my head again. *Muuhahaa!* I explained our half-quart dilemma. Eric paused for a brief moment only. I told you this guy was sharp. I sat breathlessly on the other end of the line and watched just a single drop of pink fluid drip down into the bilge before he snapped to.

"Catch it," he said.

Catch it? I thought. *Did he really just say that? With what, my hands?*

"Catch it," I repeated, slowly, involuntarily.

"Yeah," Eric said. "Find something to capture the fluid, preserve it and pour it back in. Keep it clean and you'll be fine."

Catch it, I thought again. Find a way to save those little pink drops of gold and pour them back into the transmission and "we'd be fine," according to Eric. That made sense. Reduce, reuse, right? Capture and pour back in. I could handle that. I nodded slowly and gave Eric the old "mmm-huh" as my inner gears started spinning and a little more rust dust fell to my shop brain floor. I relayed the news to Phillip, who responded with a blank, mind-boggling stare. "Do what?" he asked. I laughed a little when I saw his expression because I knew. I knew I could do this. I'd had my teeth pulled with pliers. I'd fixed a chair with Loctite. My dad had mended my alien wasp bite with tabackey juice and a Maxi pad. *I could totally do this!* Thankfully for Phillip, for the boat, and for that damn transmission, I grew up country. That's right, *country.* If there's one thing I learned on the farm, if you can't get there in mud boots or fix it with duct tape, it's probably not worth it. I'm a wizard with duct tape. It's so durable and cheap, too. Like me! A brilliant combination. I was totally going to do this. *Hand me that screwdriver. I need to start my car.*

I watched Phillip knock back a sip of water from a Dasani bottle and my jerry-riggin' instincts kicked in.

"Phillip, I'm going to need that Dasani bottle," I said sternly, ignoring his confused stare. "And some duct tape."

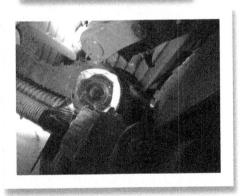

I cut the top off of the Dasani bottle and flipped it over, spout down, to make a funnel into the bottle and taped it on—real high-quality engineering. Then I taped that contraption up under the shifter arm of the transmission where the drip was coming from so the drops would fall into my custom Dasani catch bin (patent pending). The fluid then pooled in the bottle and—*voila!*—we were now successfully "capturing" the leaking transmission fluid and were able to pour it back into the transmission every half hour or so.

Nothing to it. Just takes a little country ingenuity is all. And some duct tape.

SEVENTEEN

Team Docking

With the transmission "recycle" system in place, we could finally take a breath and kick back and enjoy the passage, intermittently at least. The drip was pretty steady and Dasani bottles just aren't that big, so they were filling pretty quickly. And I'll tell you one thing duct tape adhesive does *not* like is heat. The hotter it got down there near the engine, the gummier and gooier and less adhering our adhesive became. The more I kept sticking pieces in the same place, the less they stuck. So the catch-bin needed constant monitoring when the engine was running. Then about every thirty minutes or so we had to cut the engine to let her cool so I could pull out the Dasani bottle, check the level, dump the captured fluid back into the transmission through a funnel, then pull the dipstick to make sure she was nice and coated.

I would then tape the empty catch bottle back up and start the whole process again. And I guess because the engine just happened to be in the kitchen'ish area—under the sink that is—the whole bottle-catch-dump job fell on me. That's right. Phillip had me right where he wanted me—cooking, cleaning and fluid-catching in the kitchen.

"Make sure you change the oil down there too, honey, before you make me a sandwich," he would joke.

"Yes, dear!"

Phillip really domesticated me on that trip.

The wind started to pick up after lunch and we were finally able to kill the engine. My God, what a glorious feeling. She sputtered and rattled to a stop and then it was just quiet—*so* quiet. All you could hear was the wind whistling through the sails and the splash of the water on the hull as the boat sliced through the Gulf. We had a great sail that afternoon. The wind was blowing around twelve to fifteen miles per hour and had clocked around more south southeast which helped ease us around Cape San Blas, running mostly or on a broad reach.

Unfortunately the wind is a fickle wench and she soon cranked up to about eighteen to twenty as we sailed into the night. The waves were about three to four and the boat was cooking. We were doing about six to seven knots all night, particularly while I was holding the wheel. Thankfully I had been seasoned well during our initial Gulf Crossing that these light, eighteen-miles-per-hour winds and following three-foot waves were *nothing* compared to the rough conditions we had weathered previously, particularly without the heavy heeling and the screeching dinghy banging around on the back. Although it was

overall a comparatively smoother sail, with the heavy winds it did take some muscle to hold our course. I didn't think you could get tired just holding the wheel of a sailboat but, once again, I was proven wrong. The muscles in my biceps began to cramp and complain halfway through my second shift that night but I kept at it. I stood my post for two night shifts that evening. Phillip and I traded off every two hours and I was proud to see Phillip actually fell asleep a couple of times–still right next to me in the cockpit–but this time with both eyes closed and snoozing away. I sat up in the cockpit, guiding us through the night, listening to Delilah, and belting out sappy love songs under my breath for hours on end. It was grand. I was doing it–really sailing the boat with Phillip. Just the two of us.

Having fought the wind all night we were pretty beat the next morning. Unfortunately the wind turned right on our nose as we were coming into the pass so we had to do some motoring into Panama City. That meant more transmission fluid-monitoring for Annie. We pulled into the pass around 9:00 a.m. and got ready to dock her. I really was nervous this time. This was only our fourth time docking our boat–ever. The first time was in Clearwater when I'd missed the stern pole and the corn-fed country boys had held us, red-faced, off the dock. The second was in the Carrabelle River, where the water was glass and we had Mitch. The third time–I'm not sure you would really even call it a "docking," *per se*–was when the engine cut out in the Carrabelle River and we had to throw out a bloody anchor and throw a line to the Catamaran guy to help walk our broke-down boat to the dock. That doesn't really count. Now this time, our fourth, was going to be a true two-person docking. Just Phillip and me. No Mitch, no anchor, no country boys and no corn (if that would help).

Phillip had told me many times before: "If you really want some entertainment, you should watch other boaters try to anchor or dock." It's highly entertaining, particularly when it's a couple and particularly when they're a mouthy bunch. Watching others dock is now a favorite past-time for Phillip and me. If we're kicked back in the cockpit at a marina and we see some big trawler coming in and hear the Captain shout: "Now Linda, be sure to tie the springer line first this time!" (emphasis on first), our ears perk and we elbow each other and silently nod toward the trawler because we know we're about to get a show. First off, trawlers are huge. They need lines running from every direction to hold them in place. Second, we know we've got a couple–a highly vocal Captain and a poor Linda somewhere who's scrambling for lines. We also know this is not the first time they've docked together because apparently Linda didn't tie the right line *first* last time and the Captain was displeased. He then shouts: "And make sure to do a cleat hitch, re-*mem*-ber!"

Poor, poor Linda. A cleat hitch isn't hard. It's just around a couple of times, some swoop loops on each end, and pull tight–that's how I've programmed it into my mind at least. Sadly though it seems dear Linda had been struggling with it. Phillip and I now smile slyly at each other when a scene like this pulls up. This scenario is fraught with potential. We are definitely watching but also standing ready to hop up and grab a line if Linda looks like she's going to botch it. Everyone loves a good show but no one loves to see a boat hit the dock. It's heart-breaking, like watching a little dog try to cross a busy road. No one wants to watch that. Most fellow boaters, no matter where you go, will always take a moment and offer to catch a line if they see a boat coming in. It just makes it a thousand times easier to dock and saves everyone from having to watch that poor puppy get creamed in the fast lane.

Well this was going to be our first time to dock together. I don't know if it was obvious from the dock that it was our first time–because Phillip and I aren't shouters–but I'm sure my rampant scrambling, knot tying, and visible fretting were some kind of cue. Phillip gave me the best instruction he could: "Watch the wind to see which way it's pushing the boat, hop off and catch a cleat on the leeward side." Yes, that's the best instruction Phillip could give. He can sometimes be a little technical and a little stern when he's barking orders from the *stern*. It's understandable, though, because he is stressed. I get it. He's driving the boat in. He needs a first mate who just knows what to do, not one that has to ask a bazillion questions. Thankfully he has that *now* but he did not have that then.

Then I couldn't tell for the life of me which way the wind was pushing the boat–if there even was wind–and I had no clue which side was leeward. *Leeward? Really?* I had barely wrapped my head around port and starboard at that point. I was freaked. Phillip had the wheel and I had about three lines tied to different cleats all over the damn boat, ready to tie her any which way. Phillip started to pull her into the slip and I, ready as ever, Little-Mate-that-Could, jumped off the boat prepared to tie anything. Tie anything. Tie. *Dammit!* I had jumped off the boat without a line in hand. *Brilliant!* I stood on the dock knowing I had just royally screwed up.

"Okay, now tie that bow line on the … " Phillip shouted but as the words came out of his mouth he looked up and saw my empty, useless hands, holding not a dock line–a beautiful, woven, boat-saving dock line–but rather, merely held up, empty, in the most apologetic of shrugs. I was worse than Poor Linda. All I could see were the whites of Phillip's eyes as I stood there helpless, useless, while the boat continued her steady, forward creep toward the dock.

Thankfully the good folks of Panama City must have witnessed my shameful lineless leap and they came running. As the boat lurched into the slip, an old salt came running down the other side of the dock (apparently the side I *should* have jumped off on) and had Phillip throw him a stern line. Pulling it toward him, he told me to jump back on the boat and toss him the bow line, which I did. I then jumped off–this time with a springer line in hand–and got us nice and secure. *Whew!* No crashed boat, no dock wreckage, and Phillip's eyes finally returned to normal. After an hour or so. Well, technically after a drink or three. Mortified for having played the role of "Let-Down Linda" for the day, as soon as we were showered up and back on the boat, I promptly made Phillip a smashing good cocktail. I had also stopped by the marine supply store on the way back and picked up a couple bottles of transmission fluid for our last leg home. When Phillip returned I told him, again, how sorry I was for screwing things up. *Jumping off without a line. What a stupid move.* Maybe I wasn't quite salty enough yet, I told him, as I scooched the transmission fluid bottles across the table–my makeshift apology present that I had wrapped together stupidly with a little 550-cord bow.

"Listen," Phillip started. "I don't know another sailor who could have come up with that little transmission contraption as quick as you did. You saved us out there. I think you're salting up just fine," he said as he brushed an imaginary flake or two of it off of my shoulder and smiled at me. I looked down at my shoulder instinctively as if I would actually see some there and tried to hide a goofy side-smile from him as I took a sip of his drink.

"But do try to jump off *with* a line next time, alright?" he said over his shoulder, a light tease in his voice, as he began to pull out some pots and pans to cook us dinner.

"Got it. And, you be sure to cook up that sausage just how I like it," I told him jokingly, thinking perhaps I had, in turn, done a little domesticating of the Captain during these passages as well. We seemed to make a good team: Phillip and I. I'm a sturdy, resourceful sailor–albeit an occasional screw-up–but a hard worker, always armed

with a quick wit and good humor, even in the thirtieth hour of a long, wet uncomfortable passage at sea. Phillip is a smart, technical, put-together Captain devoted to research, troubleshooting, and self-taught solutions. And he's appreciative, it seems, of the occasional humor and the company of someone who shares his avid sense of adventure. Somehow it just works.

I smiled to myself as I was setting our little pop-up table in the cockpit. *Table for two please?* I said to myself as I laid each fork on a folded paper towel. We plated up our dinners in silence, both of us thinking the same thing. We knew we were definitely going to be able to do this cruising thing. We were going to take that beautiful boat out to sandy beaches, local anchorages and exotic places. Phillip and I could handle her. We could sail her just the two of us and whatever small mistakes we were making along the way, we were learning all the while. The more we got out there and broke things, or had things break on us, the more we discovered about our boat and our own seemingly capabilities. Simply put, the more calamities we survived, the more prepared we were to handle the next inevitable malfunction. I mean, it's a boat. Something's always going to go wrong. It's how you handle it that matters. We knew that despite everything we'd been through, we hadn't yet acted like Captain Cuss and Poor Linda. We also knew we'd weathered some pretty serious conditions together—the harrowing Gulf Crossing, the hacking off of our precious dinghy, the long nights at the helm, and now the transmission fiasco. And we had pulled through them all just fine. Phillip and I certainly were no expert sailors yet but we could at least say, at that point, we had survived a violent shove in

that direction. It started with a martini, a cosmo, and a grand tale about sailing the Grenadines and it had now come to this: a 93.46% perfect boat, an epic Gulf Crossing, a custom Dasani fluid-catch, and a world full of oceans to travel with me, the rough-and-tumble, resourceful mate and him the calm and clever Captain. It was definitely going to work. These were the thoughts that filled our minds while we sat in our living-room-comfy cockpit in the marina in Panama City, looking out at the sunset, eager to make our last passage home.

EIGHTEEN

Best Sail of Our Lives

"Just one more piece of tape," I told Phillip as he was helping me strap in a fresh Dasani catch-bin for the transmission before we cranked her the next morning to motor out of the Panama City Pass. Now could we have just let her drip freely into the bilge since we now had several back-up bottles of transmission fluid to pour in? Sure. But where's the fun in that? Plus we didn't want to fill our bilge unnecessarily with gooey, tainted transmission fluid. Let engine fluids pour freely into the bilge of our boat? No sir. If we allowed it to just drain down, we would have to pump it out and wipe it out or otherwise clean it. "Might as well prevent it at the outset," Phillip said. *He's a smart man, that Phillip.* Plus the catch-bin maintenance really wasn't that bad now that we were used to it. Imagine the folks that used to get out in the cold and crank their old Model-T Fords with an actual crank through the front grill. Do you think they cared? Shoot no! They had a Model-T to cruise around in. Life was grand! So, we decided not to take the lazy man's way out and keep capturing and recycling the transmission fluid in order to keep the bilge clean. It was just a twenty-four-hour run to Pensacola anyway, so: "Might as well keep it up," as Phillip would say.

We brewed up a bit batch of coffee and headed out around 7:00 a.m. the next morning, our sights set for Pensacola. The seas that morning were calm, playing around the boat like they were trying to pull us home. We were able to kill the engine mid-morning and sail through lunch. Afterward, I went topside to bask on the deck for a bit–let the sun soak through my eyelids and just breathe in the beauty of the sail–and after a few minutes, I heard Phillip's footsteps coming toward me. He had brought our canvas hinged chairs up to the deck and handed me a gorgeous pink drink. I eyed him suspiciously, taking my drink with a frown and a quizzical stare. *He wasn't behind the wheel? He was going to sit topside alongside me while we sailed along? He was drinking? On a passage? What the?* Sensing my confusion, he explained. Well, in his Phillip way.

"Following seas make all the difference, huh?" he asked.

Following seas? Sure, they make for a smoother ride. But, I was starting to think now they meant no one had to man the helm and we got to both ride topside, side-by-side, sipping cocktails when we have following seas? *Sweet!* I said nothing. I just nodded, curled my lips in and bit down, afraid to question him and lose my rum privileges. He knew I was playing coy, so he finally explained–in Annie speak.

"It's fine if the seas are calm," Phillip said patiently. "I can set the autopilot and we can both sit up here for a bit. You just have a keep a lookout and check the GPS every once in a while. That's all."

I was nodding sweetly but still saying nothing. He knew why.

"And only one drink on passage. Just one," he said.

That finally burst my dam. "Oh, okay, great! That's awesome. I mean, one is … fine. *Totally* fine. It's so good. Thank you. I just can't believe you're sitting up here with me, both of us and we're just sitting up here. Sailing along." I was gushing, talking in those frantic, short clipped sentences I had the morning before my very first sail. Fifty words to his ten. *Is this what sailing could really be like?* I thought to myself. *So long as the seas are calm and we're cruising along safely, we can both sit topside, watch the view, take in the sunset and even—don't say it if you don't mean it—have a drink? Shut the front door!* I was floored. Of the meager but respectable cruising I had done—four hundred nautical miles and three overnight passages—this was the first time sailing felt 100% relaxing. I thought if *this* is what people imagined it would always be like when they thought about buying a sailboat and cruising, they were going to be sorely disappointed when they found themselves manning the helm in pelting rain and four- to six-foot seas, or dumping a puke bucket over the side and rinsing it out, or hanging onto the mast for dear life while trying to tie down the main, or—on the rare occasion—reaching in elbow-deep in engine heat trying to tape up a transmission fluid catch-bin. I felt instantly grateful for everything I had been through already on the boat. Sure it wasn't the full gambit of the cruising lifestyle, but I felt like it was a damn good smattering of the many varied experiences cruising can offer—particularly the one I was experiencing now—sharing a sweet, fruity drink on the bow of the boat, drenched in sunlight, my fingers woven into Phillip's, just sailing along. If this is how it could be, even just *some* of the time, it was totally and completely worth it. And, I would like to think the Cruising Gods had somehow sensed my revelation, because they decided to grace us on that last leg of the harrowing passage with what Phillip and I still call to this day—with a dreamy look in our eyes and just the faintest hint of a tear—the best sail of our lives.

Light, two- to three-foot waves lulled and pushed our boat, and the water was a soft, denim blue. It was a beautiful, sunny May day and we spent most of the afternoon basking up on the foredeck and watching the horizon. The water was so clear in some areas I felt like I could see straight through to the bottom. At one point five, maybe seven dolphins came swimming up and around the bow of our boat, rolling around on each other, playing, jumping and diving. I plopped belly-down on the deck, squealed and laughed and watched them,

thinking absolutely nothing of my camera. There was no need to film or photograph it, I was right there *living* it. Around noon the wind picked up to about ten to twelve knots, south southwest. The sails filled and never moved. We stayed on that tack for sixteen hours. Six. Teen. We barely had to hold the wheel the sails were so balanced.

We set the auto pilot–whom Jack had lovingly named "Otto" on the control panel and the name stuck–and he did all the work. Even Phillip said he had never been on a tack that long. It was incredible. The sea state started to pick up into the evening but it stayed on the same angle–south southwest–which only meant we went faster but we remained perfectly balanced, still gliding right along on our path with the helm needing only intermittent supervision.

Around 10:00 p.m., we saw fireworks on the horizon–just tiny little dots exploding above the water. We thought it might have been Destin, although we weren't sure. But it didn't matter where they were coming from, in our minds, they were for us: our own little private fireworks show in the now blissful black of the Gulf. And the moon that night was exceptional. It was bigger and brighter than I had ever seen it before, with defined crevices and craters crawling all over it. It felt like we had a beacon spotlight pouring into the cockpit all night long. We felt like those teenagers who get busted fooling around in the backseat in the school parking lot when the cop comes up and shines a blinding light through the window. *Nothing to see here officer,* I thought to myself with a chuckle. We kept turning around out of habit to see what big ass barge was coming up on us with that blinding light but it was just the moon. It was shocking how clearly we could see

everything. I could hold up my hand and see every little wrinkle in the middle of the night. It was a little cool so we were wearing our fleeces. We huddled up with some mugs of hot tea and just sat, letting the sound of the wind blowing through the sails entertain us—no incessant chatter, no small talk, and especially no freaking Delilah.

We neared Pensacola Pass around 4:00 a.m. and I'll tell you—aside from the time I jumped off the boat without a line—I've never seen Phillip's eyes light up like that. He looked like a little boy about to get a big cotton candy at the fair—sticky little fingers outstretched, hopping on one toe. He was finally *home*, sailing his boat in waters he recognized. I'll never forget his face when he saw the Pensacola Lighthouse. It was neat to think this was the same lighthouse that had been bringing sailors into the pass for over a century. With the lighthouse guiding us, we came into the pass and started making our way home, having agreed that passage would forever be the best sail of our lives. Everything had been so perfect.

It was a bit disheartening when we had to pull off of that beautiful, glorious sixteen-hour tack, but we had to crank the engine to make it into the pass and across the bay. Yes, the engine, the root of all evil! But it was the first time we'd had to crank it in about a twenty-hour passage so, all-told, it was worth it for that perfect sail. From here we would have to motor our way toward the marina. After we had made it a good ways across the bay and were nearing the marina, I went down to check on our catch-bin. Unfortunately she was filling up quickly. I know, the damn transmission again—could it *be* anything else? In order to dump the "caught" fluid back into the transmission, we needed to kill the engine and let her cool for about ten minutes before I could touch the bolt to the transmission chamber to pour the fluid back in. Unfortunately (again) we really didn't have ten minutes of room to float through aimlessly. The wind was not working in our favor in the bay and we needed the engine to keep us on track toward the entrance to the marina. We had to have a motor running but our captured fluid was inching closer and closer to the top. I watched it teeter near the lip, clocking the speed of the drops, and trying to guess how much time we had left.

"I think we've got about five minutes left on this bottle," I hollered up to Phillip.

"Alright. We've got about ten minutes left to go," he hollered back. *Gulp.* Well, at least I knew how to hide a spill. Just as Bobby had done for me with the pom-poms during my pee incident, I shoved thick wads of Brawny in and around the Dasani bottle in hopes of catching any overspill while we docked. It was a mighty fine 'sorbent pad if I do say so myself. I then ran topside to help Phillip start tying dock lines and get ready to dock the boat, telling myself: *You've got this, Annie. You can do this. Do not fuck this up!* I was nervous but something felt different. I felt like I'd been through quite a bit in my relatively short sailing career and docking had, so far, been my one serious downfall. I craved redemption. I *deserved* redemption. "You can do this!" I said out loud.

My heart was beating and thumping and felt like it was going to burst right out of my chest. I imagined it splatting in a bloody puddle, ducking its piddly heart tail and thumping its way right over the rail and into the water. *Go on. Get out of here you bloody coward,* I thought. *Who needs you?* My hands were all sweaty and I kept stubbing my toe on things as I scrambled to tie lines and hang fenders, all the while chanting: "You can do this. You can do this." We were planning to just tie up at the fuel dock for a couple of hours while we waited for the marina office to open so we could get her moved to a formal slip. Our first plan once we got the boat to Pensacola was to have it hauled out for a bottom-job–cue Bottom-Job Brandon who had rescued us with the quick crucial estimate during the survey/sea-trial. We knew the bottom work would take a couple of weeks, so we didn't yet have a permanent slip lined up. We were pulling in around 6:00 a.m. and we figured the dockmaster would show up around 7:30 or 8:00 a.m., so the fuel dock was the best option at the time.

The wind was blowing about twelve to fifteen miles per hour out of the east, which meant it was blowing us right off of the dock. *Another hairy docking? Of-fucking-course!* As Phillip began pulling the boat up alongside the dock, the wind kept pushing us off and the gap between the bow (and even the midship) and the dock kept widening. I just couldn't make the leap without losing a limb or two or my teeth when I hit the dock on the way down, assuming I even made it to the dock. And while I may have pulled a few baby ones out with pliers and strings tied to doorknobs, I was kind of fond of all of the adult ones I had now and hoping to keep them planted securely in my head. I stood at the bow, a line clenched tight in my hand this time–I wasn't going to make *that* mistake again–but it was just too far to jump. I didn't know what to do. This time I hadn't screwed up yet, I just didn't have any viable option. And, it was Phillip, this time, who got creative and took a chance. I watched in horror as he leapt out of the cockpit, the only part of the boat closest to the dock, and tied a stern line quick to a cleat. Now I was on the boat alone, with the bow pulling further and further away from the dock.

"Toss me a line," Phillip thundered from the dock. "Throw it hard!"

I wadded up a fat roll of dock line in my hand and hurled with all my might. The line stretched and unfurled toward Phillip in slow motion. It reminded me of that "floater" scene from the *Rookie of the Year* movie. Just imagine the dramatic Hollywood score playing in the background, the escalating symphony, the breathless moment and the bright clang of the cymbals as Phillip caught the tail end of the line. Trumpets blared! *I had done it! I did not fuck it up!* He pulled the bow of the boat–*and me!*–closer to the dock and told me to go back to the stern and kill the engine. When I did the silence of the moment suffocated us. Everything was suddenly so inordinately quiet. There was no motor running, no shouting, no water or waves. Just silence–and safety. Phillip and I just sat for a minute on the dock, staring at her in disbelief. There she was, our boat, tied to the dock in Pensacola. She was safe and secure. She was home. We had finally done it.

NINETEEN

The Joys of Boat Ownership

"Plaintiff's Rest. That's capital 'P' Plaintiff, apostrophe 's' then Rest, capital 'R' -e-s-t. Plaintiff's Rest."

I was spelling out the new name for the boat to the gal at the decal shop so she could give me a quote for printing and application. What was once *Fox Fire*–a perfectly good name for a boat–was soon to become *Plaintiff's Rest*–a perfectly awesome name for a lawyer's boat. I was told Phillip had been planning on christening his first boat with this name for years. His buddy from law school told me he used to talk about it even back then–the day he would get his own sailboat and call it "Plaintiff's Rest." *Sigh*. It is a great name for a floating marine haven–a nice little spin on the moment when the plaintiff finishes putting on his case-in-chief at trial, so he then rests, as well as a place for Phillip, primarily a plaintiff's attorney, to get away in when he wants to rest. It took some time, though, to explain it to the gal on the line. Like that boat we had taken out for my first sail, it seemed boats named after something nautical, then something evoking nautical action–Gulf Striker or Sea Blazer and the like–were far more common. *Plaintiff's*

Rest didn't really fit that bill, but it was our boat now, so we were free to name it as we pleased. The new decal, though, was far from free.

"$500? Seriously?" I asked in disbelief, because I really didn't believe it. The decal was going to cost around $75, but the Decal Gal was telling me the application and labor to actually stick it to the boat was going to bring the sum total to $500? *C'mon.* I had sort of befriended her with the whole Gulf Striker bit and, it seemed—much like the big greasy mechanic in the back of the shop who sold me the "start screwdriver" for my Ford Escort—she took some pity on poor me and decided to help me out.

"I tell you what Darlin'. The decal is going to run you $75, but you can stick it on yourself with a little soap and a credit card. I promise. It's not that hard," Decal Gal said.

Some soap and a credit card? Hot damn! That sounded like a Dasani bottle and duct tape solution to me.

"You got a deal," I told her and lined it up.

We'd had our boat hauled out the day after the *Rookie of the Year* docking at the fuel dock in Pensacola so our buddy Bottom-Job Brandon could do, well, the *bottom-job* on it. He was Perdio Sailor, Inc. and ran his boat repair business out of the Pensacola Ship Yard. Thankfully, the potential water leak near the strut joint for the propeller we had discovered during the survey/sea-trial turned out to be far less invasive than we had originally thought, so it was a fairly easy repair. Brandon actually said he was shocked that the fiberglass coating on the hull was so deep. It took him so long to sand down to the balsa core, he almost didn't believe there *was* one. It stood as a reminder to us how well-built our boat really is and how capable she would be of taking us across oceans and to distant shores. With the boat up on the hard, we decided to christen her with her new name on the stern so the next time she would hit the water, she would splash officially splash her as our very own *Plaintiff's Rest*.

The Decal Gal was right, too. It wasn't that hard. Some soap, a credit card, and Brandon's patent-pending "eyeball method" for leveling, and our new name was on the boat in a single afternoon.

While I focused on the really important job of the *Plaintiff's Rest* decal, the Bottom-Job boys did all of the other less-important stuff–located and sanded out all of the water blisters on the hull, checked all the thru-hulls to make sure they were clear and fully-functioning, ran through all of the systems and checked the electronics, gave the

plastic rub rail an acetone rub-down, polished up the stainless steel stanchions and pulpit, removed what was left of the warped, worn davits that caused us to lose the dinghy in the middle of the Gulf, and gave her a complete top-notch *ten coats* of paint on the hull. You got to protect that bottom! After all of that, she was ready to make a splash!

Now either because I'm the First Mate on the vessel, or the only lady that would be in attendance for the splashing (probably the latter), I was told I was going to be the one to smash the bottle on the hull for the re-naming ceremony. While I was flattered, I was also a little nervous. Phillip made a big deal out of telling me what bad luck I would bestow upon the ol' *Rest* and all of her progeny if the bottle didn't break–into a million pieces!–on the first swing. *A million!* He was very specific about the million. At first I thought Phillip was just having fun pulling my chain but after some official Google research it turned out to be true–although I do think Phillip was getting a bit too much pleasure out of my plight. I knew I had to get serious about this bottle-smashing though. I headed to the store that night and scooped up a dozen bottles of champagne–some for sipping and others for practice smash-swings on steel poles, park benches, and road signs all around town. I was going to be sure *my* bottle scattered into oblivion when she struck the hull. I had to be ready!

In the early hours of a crisp June morning, we all gathered to splash our boat for the first time as the *s/v Plaintiff's Rest*. Bottom-Job Brandon gave her one last run-through, checked all the seacocks and thru-hulls and made sure she was ready for the water. Phillip and I checked all the fluids, including the transmission fluid–*of course!*–and made sure she was ready to crank once she hit the water. Then she went, up in the straps, ready to be christened! Phillip looked about as proud as I've ever seen him–watching his boat, his dream, his vision, hovering right in front of him, finally a reality. We both walked alongside her, broad smiles and big chests, pointing, nudging and whispering to each other: "That's our boat!"

Our Broker-Turned-Buddy Kevin and Bottom-Job Brandon–both avid sailors themselves, and having owned and lived on and around sailboats for years–knew what it felt like for us to put *our* boat in the water for the first time. They brought us champagne to break and drink, slapped us on the back, and shared our excitement.

"You're going to spend your best days on her," Kevin told us.

"I hope to spend every day on her," Phillip replied.

They brought her over the water and dipped her down just low enough for me to smash the bottle on the bow. Then it was time for the big moment–you know, plagued for all eternity and what not. But I was ready. I'd been practicing. I wasn't going to let that bottle bounce back unscathed. *Uh-huh, no sir, not on this boat.* I reared back and smacked her good. Cymbals clanged and trumpets blared. Again! The bottle smashed into 932 pieces, approximately, and champagne went everywhere!

Then there was blood.

I didn't notice it at first–in all my flailing and flaunting–but Brandon did I'm surprised I didn't get it on my white shirt. I can't keep a white shirt clean to save my life. But, she was gushing. That bottle obviously found a way to get back at me. A nice shard of it jammed right into my knuckle upon impact. Perhaps I swung a *little* harder than was necessary. *Me? Overdo it? Never!* It was totally worth it though. The bottle shattered and *Plaintiff's Rest* was assured a long, lucky life at sea. We wrapped my bloody appendage and hopped on board while the boys eased her out of the dock. *Plaintiff's Rest* was back in the water!

In accordance with the necessary splash ceremony proce-dure–which we had rightfully Googled and printed out for this moment–we called upon Poseidon and the four Wind Gods (north, east, south and west), read the script to them out loud, poured generous amounts of champagne overboard in each direction–and drank generous portions ourselves–in honor of the Gods, of course. Before long we had the canvas up and we were sailing her again. *Our*

boat, this time donning her glorious *Plaintiff's Rest* title, was once again sailing home. We had a lot to celebrate!

But we didn't get to celebrate for too long. It was just a short half-hour jaunt from the shipyard to the marina and we soon had her back home, tied up in her very own slip, where the *real fun* owning a sailboat began. What's that you might ask? The work! All the dang work. Owning a sailboat is a lot of effin work. Every single laborious task is worth it, sure, but there's no getting around it: it's a lot of work. We checked on her every day, always stopping by the boat to get something, leave something, turn on something, turn off something, make sure she was getting power, make sure the bilge wasn't filling, make sure—everything, you name it. It became a daily routine. We also made a monstrous list of big and little projects, chores

and undertakings we wanted to accomplish on the boat that summer. We knew there would be a couple dozen things we would want to do to her the minute we got her back home but we hoped, once those were accomplished, the projects would dwindle down to just routine maintenance-type things. Knock on wood. But the initial list, which we began formulating somewhere between Carrabelle and Panama City, grew by the day. Much to Phillip's dismay, many of my items on the list involved hot glue, staples, and duct tape. But some really were game-changers. First there was the trio of Chair-Wow creations!

"Now you see it," I would tell people as I showed them a picture of a plain old green camping chair and then point to the boat and say, "Now you don't."

Seeing their stumped faces, I usually had to point it out. Rather than use the $45/yard outdoor UV material to make UV covers for various items on the boat the right-and-proper way, I opted to snip,

nip, tuck, and hot glue a cheap camping chair and turn it, Transformer-style, into multiple useful items on the boat. I lovingly named it the "Chair-Wow" in honor of that freaky-looking Sham-Wow guy who sold a shit-ton of those magic shammy wipes back in his infomercial heyday.

"Incredible, right?" the Sham-Wow guy would say.

"That is incredible," his infomercial sidekick, Buy-Anything-Bob, would reply. " I can't believe it. Where did the chair go? Tell me more Shamson!"

"Certainly Bob. You see, while the Chair-Wow may look like a regular old, fold-up camping chair, once you start hacking away on it, you'll find it's actually an incredible resource for many handy boat accessories, such as a Life-Sling cover for your stern rail. Or, how about a boot cover for your mast? You can even use it for smaller items, like a Velcro pouch cover for your solar cockpit lights. The uses are endless, Bob!"

"And, for only $6.95, or four easy payments of $1.73, you too can acquire the Chair-Wow at your local Home Depot or other outdoor furniture store and make all of these handy, colorful, home-made UV-protectant covers and pouches yourself."

Needless to say, I had a lot of fun with it. Other projects, however, were a lot more work than fun–like the power cord cover, which plagued me for weeks. I bought a crap-ton of stretch fleece material–green to match the other covers on the boat–cut it into little strips and then tried to staple them all together to make a fifty-foot long cover for the power cord on the boat. I thought I was doing good by stapling it inside out, like my old Cracker Barrel pants, and then turning it right-side out–you know, hide the staples and all–but it was just too small in some areas and couldn't make it around the big power cord head. It kept ripping and snagging–little staple arms and legs sticking out all over the place–like anyone would really want to grab it and roll it up in that condition anyway. It was a real mess. I finally scrapped the staple version, bought a new batch of fleece, borrowed a friend's sewing machine and did it right. And it turned out great. The cover matched the boat and made it look all fancy and color-coordinated when she was plugged in. I'm proud to say the matching green fleece covers for the fenders, which I made using the patented snip-and-staple method, seemed to work just fine and are still in working order today. I also polished all of the stainless down below–the faucets, fixtures and stove–until they shone like Jay-Z's rims.

The boys, once again, focused on less-important projects: changing out all four batteries in the house battery bank, cleaning up the wiring in the electronics panel and putting in a new bus bar to reduce the number of connections on each terminal. They fixed a leak at the base of the mast by injecting silicone in and around the bolt heads and re-taping the boot cover. Phillip and I also replaced all the gaskets in the cooling system as well as that damn ninety-six-cent dry-rotted gasket on the transmission shifter arm that had caused our pink trail of tears on the last leg of the trip. I helped with most of the boys' projects, but–for whatever reason–they didn't see fit to help me with mine. "Anyone want to take the glue gun?" fell on deaf ears.

Some days on the boat–in fact *many* days on the boat–you find yourself not kicked back, basking in the sun, a glistening rum drink in hand. *No.* You're greased up, crouched down, sweating, cramping, and cursing that blasted floating beast while you're doing something like changing the gaskets in the diesel engine. "Damn you boat!" you'll say. It's hot and grimy in most of those spaces and not spacious either. Cramming in behind the engine is no easy task on our boat but thankfully my days paying the bills as a contortionist in the Tuscaloosa Traveling Circus paid off. Getting in there requires a little in-and-out procedure where I squeeze, wriggle, and painfully maneuver myself out of a tiny little engine access hole in the aft-berth. I now know why they call it such. A birth is about what it felt like.

Engine work wasn't the dirtiest job we had to do on the boat though. Not by far. In fact I don't even think the word "dirty" could quite capture this one. It involves the head–the throne, the almighty porcelain God on our boat–that is supposed to take the shizz, pump it back into the holding tank on the boat, and keep it there. Unfortunately after a few months' use, ours wasn't doing that anymore so it was time to crack her open and replace her ailing parts, primarily the suction tube. Phillip and I donned our special shizz-repair apparel–little rubber surgical gloves–and set to it. First we had to suck as much of the shizz as we could out of the tube before we could pull her off. I started to stammer and stutter and question but the Captain cut me off.

"The Shop-Vac," he replied curtly. Yes, the Shop-Vac. The first step was to suck the crap out through the Shop-Vac, so we could at least hope to wrestle an *empty* tube off the toilet and out through the v-berth where it connected to the holding tank under the bed. And I wish this was some kind of interactive book, or a scratch-and-sniff at least, because I don't think words can express the glorious smell that emanated from our boat that day. As if this job could get any more

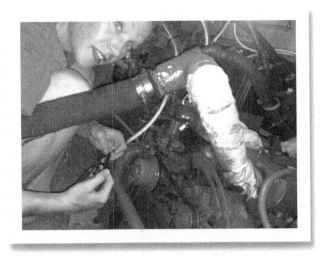

delightful, after the sucking was done, then where do you think the shizz was? Yep! In the Shop-Vac! Someone then had to clean *that* out. Where's Mike Rowe when you need him, huh? He wasn't on our boat, that's for damn sure.

You can only imagine the gentle care with which I carried that sloshing thing through the galley, up the companionway stairs, out of the cockpit, and up to the dock. I kept imagining the little plastic clamps that held the slosh-bin on were going to break at any moment and shizz would dump everywhere. Alas they held, and with the Shop-Vac purged and the suction tube cleaned out–in theory at least–we set to work on wrestling that thing off the head, which actually turned out to be a monstrous chore. *What did Phillip akin it to? Oh yeah.* Like wrestling an anaconda in an airplane bathroom. Something like that. Despite the suction wonders of the Shop-Vac, we weren't able to get *all* of the shizz out, so some of it was still oozing out while we were twisting and grappling with that stupid hose. We also now know yanking and pulling on a ripped, wire-threaded hose is not the best way to keep your flimsy, paper-thin vinyl gloves intact. It was inevitable, and it happened–as "it" often does.

I told you it was a dirty job. But while it seemed the *dirty* part was over, the *hardest* certainly was not. It took Phillip and me about two hours to maneuver, tug, pull and curse that damn hose out through the v-berth. Phillip was stationed in the bathroom trying to push and shove it through the hole in the cabinet under the sink while I was wedged under the mattress in the v-berth trying to pull it out on my end. *Damn you hose! Damn you gloves! Damn you Mike Rowe!* We were cursing anything and everything imaginable.

After we got that stinking hose out, it was really a piece of cake after that. We replaced all of the rubber parts, gave her a nice Clorox rub-down, cleaned up the last of the shizz and got her right back in working order. After that, everything went right from the toilet to the tank and stayed there. *Voila!* This job–while easily the dirtiest of jobs on the boat and yet still wildly entertaining–was not the boat chore

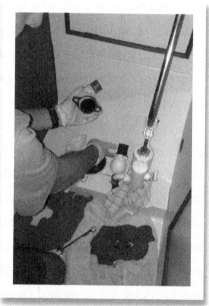

that lead to my most famous of boat project stories. *Ahhh, yes, the Story About Home Depot.* While working on boats can suck at times, other times it can serve as the absolute best fodder for writing. I swear to you every bit of this is true:

This story begins on an average Tuesday. In my pre-sailing life, I fancied myself an attorney—at least that's what the diploma said. On this particular Tuesday, I was sitting happily in court on a debt collection matter, awaiting my turn to repo a boat from some deadbeat who had stopped paying on the note. Eighteen percent on an $18,000 loan for a used fishing boat? I probably would have stopped paying too. However, he—whom we shall call Mr. Detter—thad signed the papers. He owed the debt. I was all set to win. And while Mr. Detter was a nice enough guy, I, as predicted, was the victor. I mean, he did owe the money. I was nice enough about it though. I shook his hand afterward, bid him adieu, and headed my happy self off to the Home Depot to pick up a few things for the boat in my slick court suit, my royal family french twist, and five-inch heels. I always wore five-inch heels to court.

I clacked through the store ignoring every eager, doe-eyed, orange apron-clad employee who tried to help me. "No thank you. I know exactly what I need," I would snap at them—with a hand raised to avert their cheerful efforts—as I moved swiftly through the store on the hunt for my necessities. I needed only five things: (1) a hose extender to extend our interior shower head out onto the deck; (2) a PVC plumbing fitting to connect the hose extender; (3) an outdoor rug for the dock; (4) a Shop-Vac for obvious reasons; and (5) a look at the outdoor furniture section for more potential Chair-Wow conversions. I made these rounds and grabbed what I needed quickly, waving off all assistance from the buzzing orange bees who–much like the alien wasps on the side of the interstate–continued to swarm me at every turn. I made my way up to the cash register, all ready to check out, load up my junk, and get home. However, as I hoisted the Shop-Vac onto my suit-clad hip and started schlepping all of my crap out to the car like a pack mule, I realized I didn't have my keys. *I did not have my keys.*

An exasperated sigh hissed out of me as I set all of my crap back down by the big sliding-door exit and started looking around the register, the floor around the cashier, through my bags, etc. I asked the cashier to check around her area several times for a little bunch of keys. The minimalist (and idiot) that I am, I kept my keys on one little ring: four lonely little non-descript keys on a ring. That's it. And I was looking for them in a store with a thousand little boxes of gidgets, fittings, and a million other bits that look very much like a little bunch of keys.

I started re-tracing my steps, and I say "start" because I retraced that path probably ten, twelve, thirteen times before it was all said and done that day. I headed back to the dishwasher accessory department where I had got the hose extender. No keys. The plumbing aisle where I got the PVC fitting. No keys. The rug department. No keys. The aisle with the Shop-Vacs. No keys. And, lastly, the outdoor furniture area. No keys. Everywhere I went, there were no keys. I retraced the path three more times, looking–in my suit and heels–about as "in place" as

Queen Elizabeth at a tractor pull. The orange drones, while initially reluctant to help me as I was *so* welcoming and grateful for their help initially, began to feel sorry for me and started to swarm in. I finally broke down and shared my sad plight.

"I can't find my keys."

Soon the entire floor staff knew I was the blonde who was looking for her keys. They announced it over the loudspeaker, asking several times for all employees and customers to keep a lookout for "a woman's keys." I'm not sure why the "woman" qualifier was needed. Perhaps women's keys look different than men's keys? If not, and if it was simply to emphasize the fact that a *man* wouldn't lose his keys at the Home Depot, then it still wouldn't be needed, am I right? It would be implied. Either way, the "woman's keys" bit was repeated over the loudspeaker so many times I felt they were going to offer every new customer who came through the door a "limited offer" for 20% off their entire purchase if they found this poor "woman's keys."

As I continued my repetitive trek through the store, going to the same five places 89.47 times, each orange-clad clerk that approached me would ask first, "Do you remember where you went?" I was asked that question probably twelve times, and by about the tenth, I started to respond with "No. My goodness, no. I have no idea. I've just been wandering around the store aimlessly looking in all of the places I did *not* go!" I'll admit, I was out of patience, irritated utterly with myself for having lost my damn keys and taking it out entirely on the upstanding, award-winning staff at Home Depot. I was making a real scene, turning over boxes, lifting rugs, clanging things around, looking everywhere. And still no keys. I went out to my car several times thinking maybe I left them in the ignition. No dice. If only I had still been driving that trusty red Ford Escort that started with the screwdriver, I could have simply bought a new flathead there—they had an endless supply—cranked my car and been on my merry fucking way. *If only.*

As I headed back into the store the guy in the little booth who makes key copies asked me if there was anything he could help me with. As if he didn't *know* me—the haughty blonde, haughty *woman* who had lost her keys. I decided to humor him out of spite. "Sure, I seem to have lost my keys, sir. Do you think you could help me with that?" To which he responded, completely unfazed, "Of course, ma'am. I can make you a copy. Just give me the original," he said, his stupid little cherub hand outstretched toward me. I just walked away. He wasn't worth the breath I would waste mocking him. And don't even get me started on the cashier who appeared to have the memory of a goldfish. Every time I came back to her, she would look puzzled at the fact that I wasn't holding merchandise for her to ring up and say "Can I help you?"

Yes, my keys, the keys, a woman's keys! Have you yet found or had someone turn in a set of keys? Do you recall, in any manner, that I am the WOMAN WHO LOST HER KEYS!?" I thought-screamed it but I didn't say it.

Two hours passed with me traipsing through the store, my slick "up" hairdo now shaking out in clumps and my suit jacket reeking of sweat. I decide to get scrappy. *I am going to leave here in my car dammit.*

I asked the guy in the hardware department if I could borrow a crowbar just for a minute. "I want to break into my car to make sure my keys didn't fall onto the floorboard as I was getting out." The hardware guy looked at me deadpan, not responding initially, and finally telling me he couldn't allow me to "borrow" a tool for that purpose. "Okay, fine, I'll *buy* it for that purpose. Which of these fine instruments would best serve me, sir, to break into my own car?" Realizing I was going to do it regardless, he finally handed me an old beat-up crow-bar from behind his counter.

I headed back out to my Volvo to start the exceedingly-embarrassing procedure of breaking into my own car in a suit and heels. Somehow I managed to finally push and wedge the crowbar into the sliver of a crack I had created between the door and the frame but I still couldn't reach the door lock. I was struggling and grunting and sweating and getting nowhere. I threw off my suit jacket in a huff and pushed a sweaty, blonde wad of hair from my face when I heard a voice from behind me. "Ms. Dike?" *Oh Jesus, what imminently important person could this be witnessing me in the middle of this debacle?* I could feel his eyes burning into my back. Whoever it was seemed to be gaining a large amount of pleasure from my current state of affairs.

I turned around to find the one and only Mr. Detter. *Mr. Detter? Really?* I wanted to scoff at the irony. He was smiling from ear to ear. While I may have been the victor that morning in court, he was clearly the superior now. To his credit, after a few light and well-deserved jabs–*"Look who's in trouble now?"* and *"Resorted to repo'ing them yourself now, huh?"*–Mr. Detter went dutifully to his truck and pulled out a little gismo that looked like a car antennae with a hook on the end. He said he'd used it several times to crack open his wife's car when she'd locked her keys in. He slipped it through the crack I had wedged in my Volvo and tried mightily to pull the lock up. Mr. Detter and I were out there sweating and heaving–me, in my dress and heels and Mr. Detter apparently with the wherewithal to change into work clothes before heading to the Home Depot. We were pulling on my Volvo door when another voice beckoned from behind us. "Excuse me ma'am? Sir? Can I ask you what you're doing?" I closed my eyes and cursed the Key Gods again. *What fresh new hell is this?*

It was the cops, that's who it was. Yes. A Daphne P.D. Captain Something-or-Other trying to stop two mastermind criminals–Mr. Detter and me–from stealing some good, upstanding citizen's Volvo. And, you might be thinking: *Okay, she has to be making every bit of this up. Like the cops would really just show up at that moment?* They did, and let me prove it to you–so you will never again doubt the integrity of my stories and the depths to which I will go to entertain you with my misfortunes. The cops came because the Home Depot in Daphne, Alabama is located right next to the Daphne Police Department. I kid you not. Look it up.

The whole force must have been sitting in their office–stale coffee and jelly donuts in hand–watching me go out to my car two or three times, punch it, kick it, throw my suit jacket off in protest, and finally begin trying to break into it with a Home Depot crowbar. Not an arrest-worthy offense yet, but when I solicited the everyday do-gooder, Mr. Detter, to assist me in my dirty deeds, that was it. They *had* to come investigate then. And I'm sure things didn't sit well initially with Captain Something-or-Other when I struggled to explain who Mr. Detter was and why he was helping me. I believe I introduced him initially as "my colleague" which, I agree, sounds sinister. But thankfully I think the sheer magnitude of my utter mortification began to sink in and the Captain believed I was, in fact, simply trying to break into *my own* car to find *my own* keys. Amused by my situation, he decided to pitch in. He whipped out his official car-breaker-into device–which proved far more effective than Mr. Detter's homemade version–and popped my door right open. The Captain had me sign a waiver acknowledging it was, in fact, my own car he had broken into and that I was, thereby, releasing the Daphne P.D. of any liability in connection with his act. Not knowing my occupation and me looking nothing like a put-together lawyer at the moment–all sweaty and fuming–Mr. Detter got a hearty laugh out of the cop's explanation to me that "liability" was just a fancy "lawyer word" for fault. "Sign here," he said.

But, alas, having broken into the car and signed my rights away to the Daphne P.D–all to find *no keys* in the floorboard of my car, I headed *back* into the store to once again retrace my steps through the various departments. The cashier gave me that can-I-help-you? look again as I walked in and I just held up a hand to her as I walked by. With the best of intentions, Mr. Detter asked me, "Do you remember where you went?" to which I responded, "Yes. Electrical. I spent the entire time in electrical. Will you please go check there?" just to shake free of him. I was exasperated, exhausted, and so desperate with the situation, I wasn't even embarrassed anymore. I didn't care what

I looked like. I didn't care who stared. I didn't care about anything but my keys. I stood inside the entrance, facing the vast spread of the Home Depot store in front of me, my hands placed firmly on my suit-clad hips just about ready to give up and call Triple A when a dopey orange-clad employee came up to me. "Are you the woman looking for her keys," he asked. I stood there dumbfounded for a minute, my hair sweaty and stringy on my neck, my dress smeared with grease and dirt from the crowbar and door jam and still in my heels. I mean, I had no other shoes. I nodded fervently, too frazzled to make any more snide remarks about it. I just nodded. *Yes. It is I. The woman who lost her keys.* "Here you go," he said. "Some customer found them in a box of fittings in the plumbing aisle."

There, in his meaty paw, lay my keys. *My keys! Thank the ever-loving stars in heaven!* I squealed and gripped him tight in a bear hug that pulled him right off the floor. I wondered for a second how or why I had dropped or set them down in the plumbing aisle, but not enough to go find out. I honestly did not care. I had my keys! I could leave! I hustled back to the sliding-door exit—where my crap was piled in a neglected heap—hoisted it all up on my hip and jogged out to my car, hoping Mr. Detter wouldn't see or hear me. I'm surprised they didn't announce it over the loudspeaker though. Having been so vocal over it when my keys were lost, surely they would want to spread the exuberant news that they were now found! As I shoved everything in the Volvo and climbed in, an odd sensation struck me—the cool leather of the seat on my back. *My back.*

I reached back and, sure enough, my dress was unzipped all the way down to my waist. If the shoddy hot-glue and stapled wardrobe of my Cracker Barrel days hadn't sufficiently revealed it, I am not known for owning impeccably-tailored clothes. Rather, I am the type that will squeeze into a dress two sizes too small and strap up the part that won't zip with some string, glue, ribbon, or Velcro flap I've created. Or—in this case—I will throw a suit jacket over the unzipped crevice because, surely, I won't have any reason to take my jacket off, will I? Of course I will not. *Hold your hand over the glue spot to hide it, Annie. You can do this.* Or throw a jacket over it and keep it on all day, no matter the heat, sweat or weather—a perfect solution. I now realized the entire time I had been man-handling my car, interacting with the doe-eyed Mr. Detter, and talking with the cop, my dress had been unzipped all the way down my back with my criss-cross bra peeking out for all the world to see. I am just that classy.

But the best part of this story was, when I came to Home Depot, I was irritated by my wasted morning in court, sick of being stuck in a stuffy suit, and annoyed that I had to stop by Home Depot in heels to pick up a few things for the boat. But now—*now?*—I was the happiest woman alive. I had my keys! I could crank my car! And, I could *drive* it and *leave* the Daphne effin' Home Depot forever. To this day, I have never been back to that one. I was all smiles and sunshine as I pulled out of the parking lot that day, three hours after I had pulled in—leaving Mr. Detter behind to dutifully overturn boxes in the electronics department in search of a "woman's keys." I sang every song that came on the radio all the way home. Even sappy Delilah-worthy love ballads got a peppy treatment. Nothing could dampen my mood. It took a sweaty, mortifying afternoon at the Home Depot with Mr. Detter and the Daphne P.D. to remind me: if you think your day is going badly, know that it can always get worse. I learned that lesson originally from Big Mom a long time ago, but a good crappy day can always remind me. Swig, swish, spit. "It ain't that bad. You're alive, ain't ya?" she had said.

You're damn right I am, Big Mom. And, now I have my keys!

TWENTY

The REAL Joys of Boat Ownership

All evidence to the contrary—the sweat, the glue, the duct tape, and the shizz—the numerous boat projects we did that summer were rewarding in a sense. We knew we had to get over that initial "project hump"—get those dozen or more *big* projects knocked out—before we could kind of kick back, ease into the maintenance-work-only phase, and get her out cruising in our local waters. While I don't think I would classify those initial projects as fun—entertaining, yes, but fun, no—they weren't all that bad either. In order to take the boat out and enjoy her, you have to do the work that comes with it. There's just no getting around it. But just as a long uncomfortable passage can make a tepid drizzle-shower at a truck stop feel like a deep-sea scrub at an Italian spa, hot, sweaty, tiresome boat chores can make a beautiful, breezy sail across the bay feel like the best damn day of your life. It's all about balance. Generally speaking, the more work you have to put into the boat means the more you'll get out of her, the further you'll be able to take her, and the longer you can stay when you do. The tougher the boat chore, the more sense of accomplishment and enjoyment you'll get out of it. Simply put, the more work, the more pleasure. But, what's play without work, am I right? Can one really even exist without the other? If you've never worked a day in your life, how can you ever possibly appreciate a day of play?

After the exhausting passages we had made and all the work involved in the numerous malfunctions, near-misses, and other fiascos that came along with them—not to mention the additional work we'd been doing on the boat since we got her to Pensacola—it was high time we got to playing. We had earned the right to do a hell of a lot of playing. I didn't even know yet how mind-blowingly blissful the cruising lifestyle could be. I had yet to see the real reward, the true benefit, the dreamy image that *other people* conjure when they think about buying a sailboat. I'm talking about life on the hook. I saw it as some fantasy place where the boat glides into a crystal green cove, this magical device called an "anchor" is let down, and then the boat just floats blissfully in a dreamy little inlet where dolphins and sea turtles swim. There is no heading to hold, no sails to trim, no dinghy to hack, no transmission fluid to catch. Shipyards, bottom-jobs and shitty Shop-Vacs do not exist in this utopia. I thought it was just a dream. I had no idea it could be a reality, until Phillip showed me.

Somewhere in between the stapled-power-cord-cover project and the Chair-Wow creations, we took a break from all of our working to finally take our boat out and show Little Miss Annie what it was like to spend a few blissful days on the hook. We headed out into the bay on a bright Friday afternoon, leaving the stress and toil of the work week—the office, all the emails and calls—behind us on the shore. Sure,

we weren't more than a mile from shore, but the minute the engine cut and all we could hear was the gentle luffing of the sail and the water dancing on the hull, it could have been a hundred. There's just something about heading out and seeing it all shrink in the distance behind you on the horizon that makes it feel like it's just that: *distant*.

Now that Phillip and I have done a small, but respectable amount of cruising, I have a true appreciation for the incredible cruising grounds we have here in Pensacola. We've got a huge bay with a lot of fetch, depth, and just a small scattering of buoys. Not a crab pod in sight. You can tack and jibe and just sail for sport for miles. Head east around Deer Point and you can tuck into Little Sabine and anchor out right behind all the craziness of Pensacola Beach. Or pass the Little Sabine entrance, duck under the Bob Sykes Bridge and drop your hook behind the famous Paradise Inn, where live music rolls out from the open amphitheater all the way to your boat. Head west and you'll find yourself headed toward the entrance to the pass, where you can watch big fishing boats and barges come through. Just beyond the entrance, you can take the North Cut behind Sand Island, where we usually like to anchor, out at Red Fish Point or up in the inlet, near Ft. McRae.

That first weekend Phillip took me out to Red Fish Point–a place his parents used to take him and his sister as kids to camp on the beach. After having studied all of those anchoring diagrams, learning about the all-important swing radius, and imagining the little stick sailors on their stick boat waving their stick arms in fright, I didn't have to worry about any of that, because there wasn't a single damn boat out there with us. There was no dock, no shoal, no other vessel in sight. We had the whole place to ourselves. We dropped the anchor and the boat sat blissfully about one hundred feet from the shore, with not a thing to do but bob and sway in the waves. It felt like she was sitting in a hammock–her arms folded behind her head, her feet kicked up and crossed, just swinging. She had worked harder than all of us to get here and had certainly earned the right to kick back and relax. At first, I didn't know what to do with myself. Without any work to be done, no systems to monitor and check, no cleaning, scrubbing or cooking to do at the moment, I wandered around the deck a little bewildered, until I heard an inviting kerplunk from the back of the boat. Phillip had dropped the swim ladder and set some towels in the back of the cockpit for us when we got out, because we were about to get in.

He stomped past me on the deck, slapped my ass as he ran by and hollered "Get in here!" as he jumped into water head first. I couldn't get my crappy clothes off fast enough. I scrambled out of my shorts, kicking and flailing like Runt trying to climb the cab of the pickup and jumped in after him. It reminded me of the pool back in Clearwater that Phillip, Mitch and I had so greedily jumped into after making that first passage from Charlotte Harbor to Clearwater. Something about the salt, sweat, and sunscreen on your skin feels so refreshing when you immerse yourself in a body of crisp, cool water. It's like the dirtier you are, the better feels. And, I must have been a gunked-up, mucky hot mess because the water that afternoon felt incredible. It had this rejuvenating property, like we'd jumped into some nutrient-filled fountain of youth or something, as if the water was really magical. I couldn't stop gulping big cheekfuls of air and going underwater, wiggling my way down and back up. It just felt *so* good.

I popped back up to find Phillip swimming toward shore, so I barreled after him, indulging myself in the rush of the race. Sadly he was a Scout swimmer back in the Marines so I hadn't the slightest chance but I paddled my heart out anyway, not trailing too far behind him by the time we could touch bottom near the sandy shore. We both sat in the water for a minute, catching our breath and looking back at the boat, her glimmers and glints in the falling sun feeling like playful winks and smiles at us. Just as she had that first day we laid eyes on her back in Punta Gorda, she looked so happy. She seemed to be thanking us for bringing her here. But, we were happy too! This place was incredible. As Phillip started walking across the little spit of land that separates Red Fish Point Cove from the boundless waters of the Gulf, I could hear the sand squelching beneath his feet. I felt it too when I began to follow behind him, almost tickling the soles of my feet and leaving behind soft footprints in the beautiful, sugar-white sands. The crash of the waves on the Gulf shore sounded almost like a roar as we made our way across–like the deep, breathy rumble of a packed stadium. Once we traversed the peak and the shore came into view, the waves were much smaller, but from the other side they had sounded huge.

Phillip and I walked along the Gulf shore, picking at a few shells, pointing out a dolphin or two and twisting our feet a little more with each step to make the quartz in the sand squelch a little more. It amazed me to think it was this very place, this same sandy shore that Phillip had walked as a child. I tried to picture it. He would probably be carrying a stick or something and would kick at things in the sand and run often, as kids do. And, he would have had a headful of sandy blonde hair. That part was a little hard to imagine, as his head is always clean-shaven now. But I felt proud to be here with him–back in his home waters, making his first weekend trip out to the place that held so many memories for him, this time making new ones on his very own sailboat. I had a sneaking feeling when I met him that he was destined to spend his future in a place like this–a magical utopia that I thought was just a figment of my imagination. But a small part of me, deep inside, had hoped at that time that the place was real, that it did exist, and that he would take me there. And here I was.

After our blissful dip, we patted ourselves dry in the cockpit and made two glistening rum drinks to sip on the deck while we watched the sun set over the bow. Exquisite streaks of pink, orange and blazes of yellow stretched from either horizon. They looked just as stunning in the sky as they did lighting the arc of Phillip's brow. One drink turned to two and "just a half more" before the sun finally went down and we sat there watching every hot pink minute of it.

Talk then turned to dinner–something we had been plotting, planning and salivating over all week. Planning meals for a weekend out on the boat is now one of our favorite parts of provisioning. You look forward to doing the prep work–cutting up all those colorful vegetables and greens–because you don't have anything else to do. You can lose

yourself in a heavy glass of wine and an old Commodores song while you spend the most peaceful ten minutes of your day cutting up an onion. Life is just that good. And Phillip, with his exceptional culinary skills makes it even better. If you thought living on a boat meant a full diet of canned goods, dried beans, and beef jerky, I'll have to break the sad news—the meals Phillip has made us on the boat are some of the most gourmet, exquisite, five-star immaculate feasts I have ever let pass my lips. We have made bone-in pork chops with mustard sauce, succulent peppercorn-rubbed steaks with glazed brussel sprouts, big, juicy hand-pattied cheeseburgers, bacon-infused shrimp and grits, teriyaki salmon with mushroom risotto. I could go on. And on. Most dinners I've had at fancy schmancy, super pricey restaurants pale in comparison to those I've eaten in the cozy little cockpit of our boat.

Not to mention dinner is served under a silver moon and glistening quilt of stars. The wine almost seems to glow in that setting, as do our eyes just before we pounce on the bountiful feast spread before us. Even the water glows. Jump in the salty surroundings of the Pensacola Bay in late summer and your arms and legs will light up as you swish them through the phosphorescence. In the summer, we would jump in every night after dinner—usually sans swimming attire if we were the only ones in the anchorage—which was common. Running your glowing fingers along your arms and stomach, you feel like you're on a drug. But, this is *way* better than any drug. It's life and you're there, knee-deep in it, scooping it up in juicy fistfuls and gulping it in, with absolutely no desire to be anywhere else. How often can you say that? When you're sitting at your desk waiting for five o'clock to roll around, or when you realize it's only Monday and

you're already waiting for Friday, or as you're flipping through travel brochures and websites, waiting for your next vacation. Waiting, waiting, waiting. It's sad to think how much time we spend wishing our time away–waiting for some moment in the future. Well Phillip and I were not. Not that summer at least, and not since we got that boat. Whether we were stuck cramped, cursing, and sweating through another boat project that we know will offer us another blissful, savory, satisfying phosphorescent night under the stars on her, we are *in* the moment, on that big, beautiful chore-of-a-boat.

TWENTY-ONE

About Your Boat

We savored every minute of that summer, spent every day either thinking about, talking about, or tinkering on our boat. We scrubbed her, fixed her, sailed her, anchored her, and docked her and when the summer months finally dwindled down and fall set in, we then tied her up every which way and headed off to New York City. That's when we got the call about our boat. You remember Karen, the pre-trip buzzkill, Lieutenant Whazzisname and Sergeant So-and-So, who couldn't disclose what the hell was going on with our boat—our big, beautiful, beast-of-a-boat.

Phillip and I wandered around the park in New York aimlessly, staring at his phone, trying to will it to ring with our minds while we waited for Lieutenant Whazzisname to call us back. We were offering up possible not-so-bad scenarios but internally suspecting the worst—the crashed, cracked versions. We kept turning his words over and over in our minds: "It's about your boat." How worried we were, I simply cannot disclose.

After a nail-biting ten minutes in NYC, the Lieutenant from the Pensacola Police Department finally called us back and told us they had been trying to track Phillip down back in Pensacola on behalf of the Fort Walton Police. Turns out it was actually the Fort Walton guys that wanted to talk to Phillip "about his boat." This was a very important piece of information Sergeant So-and-So could have told us seeing as how our big, beautiful expensive sailboat is not *in* Fort Walton. That wouldn't have left us imagining *Plaintiff's Rest* smashed into a pile of wood and epoxy at our dock back, you know, in Pensacola. But, apparently, he wasn't at liberty to *disclose* such vital information. With the Fort Walton hint, Phillip started to suspect that it could be about the dinghy. *The dinghy?* The thought totally threw me.

First of all I don't really even consider a dinghy to be "a boat." I mean, I guess it's a watercraft. It floats and carries people. You can paddle or motor around it. I get that. But, if our sailboat and the dinghy were tied up together in a slip, and someone said, "Hey, nice boat!," I wouldn't say, "Thanks, she's a 2001 six-seater Caribe with matching oars." I would, assume–like the rest of the world I would hope–that he's talking about the sailboat. The *real* boat. Not the *dinghy*. And why would the Ft. Walton guys be calling us about our dinghy? I mean we hacked her off the back of the boat in the middle of the damn Gulf. I imagined she had floated along finally free as a blue-jay, frolicking with the dolphins and dorados–much like the wide-eyed cat in the psychedelic cat food commercial batting at little fish-shaped pieces of meat leaping about, as happy as happy can be. Like when the family pet passes and you tell the little ones "No, honey, Brisco didn't die. He's living on a great big farm, chasing squirrels all day." I envisioned it that way because that's not the image I was left with when we sawed the dinghy off the stern of our boat and watched her float alone into the darkness over big, murky waves, existing only in the single beam of our flashlight—until we clicked it off and turned our backs on her, like making the second turn in those dark, dreary drainage pipes. That was it, right? She was gone. We had moved on. Wrong.

Our dinghy didn't float away into the abyss. She didn't retire to leaping dolphins and rainbows. No, our dinghy floated her spiteful little self all the way to Fort Walton Beach to have her revenge on us. "Cut me off of the boat will they?" she said. "I'll get those heifers!" But, having floated freely across the entire Gulf, the minute she hit shore, she ended up behind bars. Well, behind a chainlink at least. Apparently she didn't think to grab her papers before we cut her loose. *Them's the breaks!*

Someone had apparently found her in the woods and brought her in to the Fort Walton station. Thankfully we had registered the dinghy in Phillip's name before setting off on The Crossing so they were able to track her back to us. But they sure weren't in a hurry. We learned the dinghy had been sitting there, staring sadly through a chain link fence, waiting for us to come get her, since July. *July?* I thought. Yes, three months, sitting in a parking lot, out in the sun. But at least she'd made it back.

The outboard was nowhere to be found, but I'm sure that thing was toast well before she reached the shore. I remember when it crashed into the water from the davits, oil and gas flowing out of it like lava. I doubt it was salvageable. But I really couldn't believe she had come back to us. All that way. The damn dinghy. Perhaps there are a lot of

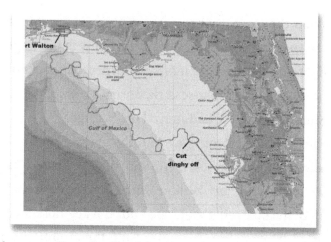

sailors who can tell a tall tale of the time they had to hack their dinghy off in the middle of a passage. *That's nothing!* But, I'm not sure there are many who can say their dinghies came back. As we hoisted her onto a trailer and strapped her in to take her home, I felt a bit of kinship to her. She had certainly endured quite a mighty passage to make it back to us. While hacking her off in the raging waves had been the pinnacle of *our* harrowing crossing, it was just the beginning of hers. Surely she'd faced, resisted, and overcome plenty of her own epic events as she charged across the Gulf after us, determined to make it. I started to wonder what stories our dinghy could tell us about her adventure. Perhaps she floated past Robert Redford in an ailing life raft, or an Indian boy and his tiger adrift at sea. Or maybe she hallucinated the entire time and *did* bat at leaping, neon goldfish. We'll never know. But, to tell you the truth, I was kind of proud of her. I saw a bit of myself in her. She had survived a lone Gulf Crossing–her first I'm sure–and she had a nice thick layer of salt on her skin to prove it.

About the Author

In a former life, Annie was a trial attorney. Six years in the practice, however, taught her two very important things: 1) she loves to write, but 2) she hates do it in a fluorescent-lit office. At twenty-nine, Annie stepped away from the practice with the clear mindset to travel, to sail, to live a different day every day and write about all of it. Annie now writes full-time and spends the majority of her days with the Captain cruising their Niagara 35 sailboat around Florida's west coast, the Keys and beyond. While *Salt of a Sailor* is her debut non-fiction piece, Annie has written and published several practice guides and other humorous and dramatic pieces and has more in the works. Check out

Annie's books on Amazon and Kindle and follow her many (mis) adventures via her Facebook posts, blogs and YouTube videos at *HaveWindWillTravel.com*.

Made in the USA
Middletown, DE
23 December 2020